REVISE AQA GCSE (9–1)
History
CONFLICT AND TENSION
BETWEEN EAST AND WEST, 1945–1972

REVISION
GUIDE AND WORKBOOK

Series Consultant: Harry Smith

Author: Paul Martin

Also available to support your revision:

Revise GCSE Study Skills Guide   9781447967071

The **Revise GCSE Study Skills Guide** is full of tried-and-trusted hints and tips for how to learn more effectively. It gives you techniques to help you achieve your best – throughout your GCSE studies and beyond!

Revise GCSE Revision Planner   9781447967828

The **Revise GCSE Revision Planner** helps you to plan and organise your time, step-by-step, throughout your GCSE revision. Use this book and wall chart to mastermind your revision.

For the full range of Pearson revision titles across KS2, KS3, GCSE, Functional Skills, AS/A Level and BTEC visit:
www.pearsonschools.co.uk/revise

Contents

• •

A small bit of small print

AQA publishes Sample Assessment Material and the Specification on its website. This is the official content and this book should be used in conjunction with it. The questions and revision tasks in this book have been written to help you revise the skills you may need for your assessment. Remember: the real exam questions may not look like this.

Aims of the key leaders

The Second World War ended in 1945. The leaders of the 'Big Three' Allied countries had to decide what would happen to Europe. But their different aims and ideas weakened the alliance, with tensions at first, then outright hostility.

The Grand Alliance

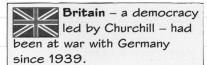 **Britain** – a democracy led by Churchill – had been at war with Germany since 1939.

The USA – a democracy led by Roosevelt – had been at war with Germany and Japan since December 1941.

 The USSR (Soviet Union) – a communist one-party state led by Stalin – had been at war with Germany since 1941.

To compare communism with the capitalist democracies, see page 2.

The Grand Alliance therefore was a 'marriage of convenience', in which three countries shared the aim of defeating their common enemy – Nazi Germany.

The USSR was made up of communist Russia and 14 other Soviet republics.

Winston Churchill

- ✓ Conservative aristocrat with traditional values.
- ✓ Strong supporter of the British overseas empire, despite rising pressure for countries' self-rule.
- ✓ Deeply suspicious of Stalin and communism.
- ✓ Determined to stop Soviet expansion.

Franklin D. Roosevelt

- ✓ Key figure in holding the Grand Alliance together.
- ✓ Prepared to work with Stalin despite differences.
- ✓ Allied with Stalin to encourage his support against Japan.
- ✓ Recognised need to accept the USSR's status as a superpower.
- ✓ More focused on building trade than on revenge.

Joseph Stalin

- ✓ Strengthened one-party rule in the USSR and restricted freedoms.
- ✓ Convinced West wanted to destroy communism.
- ✓ Determined to stand firm against the USA and Britain, and secure his eastern border.
- ✓ Refused to be 'bullied'.
- ✓ Keen to expand territory and influence westwards.

The aims of the 'Big Three'

Europe should be democratic – a capitalist democracy. This means different political parties working to win voters' support in free elections.

Churchill (left), Roosevelt (centre) and Stalin (right) – the 'Big Three' – in 1945.

Germany should have to pay reparations, ensuring that it is never strong enough to start another war.

Germany should be rebuilt to make sure Europe is stable.

Britain fought for Poland: the Polish people should be free from communist influence, and able to choose their government.

Europe should be democratic – a communist democracy. Only communism truly represents the workers, so democracies can only be communist.

Now try this

What do you think was the main aim of each of the 'Big Three' leaders? List **one** aim for each leader. For each aim, explain why this might cause tension with the other two leaders.

Attitudes and ideologies

The Allies had contrasting (different) attitudes and **ideologies**. Once the war was over, this increased tensions. The West preferred **capitalism** and the East preferred **communism** – and this divided Europe even more.

> **Ideology** is a set of political ideas about how society should be run. Understanding ideology is key to understanding the **Cold War**. The USA and the USSR had opposing ideologies.

The USA, Britain and capitalism: making money

Said communism enslaved people to the state. Capitalism was based on freedom and democracy:

- Everyone should be free to make money for themselves.
- Individuals are better at deciding what to make/sell than the state.
- Trade between countries makes everyone richer.

The USSR and communism: sharing money

Said capitalism exploited the workers to make the rich even richer. Communism was based on fairness:

- Capitalism only makes some people rich by exploiting everyone else.
- Individuals are not as strong as everyone working together for the same aim.
- The state should take control of the economy and run it to benefit everyone.

Capitalist democracy and the people

- Individual freedoms
- Multi-party free elections
- People free to decide their own fate
- Freedom of speech

Communist dictatorship and the people

- Everyone works for the 'common good'
- Single-party state
- Workers to overthrow capitalists
- Censorship and police state

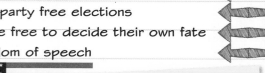

> The US flag is a symbol of freedom. The stripes represent the 13 colonies that fought for freedom from British rule.

> The flag of the USSR shows a hammer and sickle to represent the workers and peasants who rose up in revolution.

The Russian Revolution, 1917

Communism is based on the principle of a worldwide revolution: that those taken advantage of by capitalists will overthrow capitalism and work for the common good.

In 1917, communists took over the government of Russia in a bitter civil war. Capitalist powers such as the USA and Britain supported the government, but were defeated. This created distrust between the two sides.

The Red Scare

Capitalist countries were shocked by the 1917 Russian Revolution. They also feared that communist revolution would spread. The communists also pulled Russia out of the First World War, abandoning their allies.

The USA, in particular, was driven by fear of the 'Red' (communist) threat – waves of suspicion and fear of communist spies led to arrests, violence and panic across the USA.

Now try this

List **three** reasons for distrust between the USA and the USSR.

Yalta and Potsdam conferences

The Grand Alliance met at two key conferences in 1945 to plan for the future: at **Yalta** (February) and **Potsdam** (July–August). During Potsdam, both the USA and Britain changed their leaders.

Yalta, February 1945

- Germany, when defeated, would be reduced in size, divided and demilitarised. It would pay $20 billion in **reparations**: half to the Soviets.

- Europe would be rebuilt along the lines of the 1941 Atlantic Charter. Countries would have democratic elections.

- The United Nations (UN) would be set up, though only Russia and two other Soviet republics would be members.

- The USSR would declare war on Japan once Germany was defeated.

- **Tension:** Poland would be in the Soviet 'sphere of influence', with a democratic government. The position of the border with the USSR gave land to the Soviets.

The Second World War

Timeline

June 1941 Nazi invasion of the USSR.

June 1944 Allied invasion of Normandy (D-Day).

April 1945 US President Roosevelt dies.

June 1945 UN set up.

July–August 1945 Potsdam Conference.

September 1939 Outbreak of WWII.

December 1941 Japanese attack on Pearl Harbor; USA enters the war.

February 1945 Yalta Conference.

May 1945 Germany surrenders.

July 1945 Churchill replaced by Clement Attlee.

September 1945 Japan surrenders; end of WWII.

Harry S. Truman

Truman was Roosevelt's vice president. He had little experience of foreign affairs and was not involved at Yalta. He supported self-government of individual nations and international cooperation. He distrusted Stalin from the start and tried to bully him with US power. He was concerned about growing Soviet influence in Eastern Europe and believed Stalin was more interested in using force than in cooperation.

Clement Attlee

Attlee was leader of the Labour Party and was focused on rebuilding Britain. He accepted that Britain was no longer the dominant power and saw staying close to the USA as vital. Concerned with Soviet expansion, his priority was to make Germany safe from Soviet aggression.

With the war won, and his **Red Army** in Europe, Stalin was less willing to compromise.

Potsdam, July–Aug 1945

- A Council of Foreign Ministers was set up to organise the rebuilding of Europe.

- The Nazi Party was banned and war criminals were to be prosecuted.

- Germany was to be reduced in size and divided into four zones of occupation run by Britain, France, the USA and the USSR.

- Berlin was also to be divided up.

- The USSR was to receive 25% of the output from the other three occupied zones.

Yalta and Potsdam: outcomes

Remember: while Britain, the USA and the USSR were able to work together to defeat Germany, who had surrendered in May 1945, tension was increasing between the wartime allies. Differences were beginning to emerge over the future of Germany and Eastern Europe. Moreover, Roosevelt's death had led to Truman becoming president and he was much more distrustful of the USSR.

Now try this

Students often confuse what happened at these conferences. Make sure you know the differences and the similarities between them.

Explain what was agreed at Yalta and Potsdam. Write **one** short paragraph about each conference.

Dropping the bomb

On 6 August 1945, a US bomber dropped the first **atom bomb** – on the Japanese city of Hiroshima. A second bomb was dropped on Nagasaki three days later and Japan quickly surrendered. The use of this new and terrible weapon had a dramatic effect on post-war superpower relations, starting an evolution from allies to rivals and then all-out enemies.

Truman and the atom bomb

Truman deliberately delayed the Potsdam Conference until the atom bomb was ready. He thought he would get his way in the talks because of this huge military advantage.

The bomb gave Truman confidence and determination at Potsdam. It also made the countries of Western Europe confident about relying on US protection.

For more on the Potsdam Conference, see page 3.

Stalin's response

The threat made Stalin more determined to secure the USSR through a 'buffer' of pro-communist states in Eastern Europe. This was the exact opposite of what the USA hoped for.

Consequences of the bomb

The development of the atom bomb increased tensions and rivalry between the superpowers dramatically. It also made Stalin determined to close the technology gap with the USA.

However, the destruction the bomb could cause did make the rival superpowers more reluctant to go to war against each other.

Other countries were quick to get atomic weapons, too. Just four years later, in 1949, the Soviets tested their first bomb. Britain, France and China soon followed.

A nuclear mushroom cloud towers 20,000 feet over Nagasaki, 1945. Truman's secrecy over the bomb raised Soviet fears that the USSR might be the next target.

The 'Iron Curtain': allies turn into enemies

- A secret report from US ambassador Kennan in Moscow to President Truman in February 1946 claimed that the USSR saw capitalism as a threat to be destroyed. The USSR was building its military power, as peace with the capitalist USA was not possible.

- In March 1946, Churchill gave a speech in the USA about US–Soviet relations. He described an '**iron curtain**' separating East and West. He saw the USSR as a threat to world peace and freedom. This increased tensions further, as Stalin saw the speech as an unfair attack.

- In September 1946, a telegram from Novikov, Soviet ambassador to the USA, told Stalin that the USA wanted world domination and was building up its military strength. Only the USSR could stand up to it. He claimed that the USA was preparing its people for war with the USSR.

- The USA saw the USSR as a threat to its economic interests in Europe. The USSR feared and resented the USA's nuclear monopoly. Distrust had evolved into hostility.

Now try this

How did the atom bomb turn allies into enemies? List **three** impacts on superpower relations.

The division of Germany

As agreed at Yalta and Potsdam, post-war Germany was divided into four zones. The capital, Berlin, was also divided into four – despite being inside the Soviet zone of administration.

See page 3 for more on the Yalta and Potsdam conferences.

The Potsdam division

- Germany was reduced in size, losing all land gained after 1937. The eastern border was moved much further west, giving more land to Poland.
- Each of the four Allies were to administer (run) their own zones independently.
- The German economy was to be managed as a whole, with no divisions.
- The aim was to reunite Germany under one government as soon as possible.

The division of Germany in 1945.

Spheres of influence

Although nothing was ever signed to say so, the Allies agreed broadly on the spheres of influence maintained by East and West (the countries that each would support).

- **The East:** Poland, Czechoslovakia, the Baltic States, Hungary, Romania and Yugoslavia provided a Soviet **buffer**.
- **The West:** Western Europe, Greece and Italy were to remain pro-Western.

Reparations

Reparations were to be taken in materials, labour and goods from each zone. Stalin wanted to punish Germany and keep it weak. The USA wanted to help Germany recover from the war to avoid further conflict.

The Soviets controlled the poorest zone, which had much less industry. Therefore, it was agreed that they could have 25% of the industrial equipment in the other zones in return for raw materials from their zone.

Reparations are payments a defeated nation has to pay the winners to cover the damage and costs of the war.

Poland

Poland was a big problem. Stalin was keen to secure a large buffer zone against future German aggression. Returning to the borders as they were in 1921 gave the Soviets significant territorial gains at Poland's expense.

However, Britain had gone to war to defend Poland's independence and the USA was keen to limit Soviet expansion. Neither Britain nor the USA wanted the USSR to gain more ground.

Although Stalin agreed to free elections in Poland, he expected the result to be a pro-communist government. Meanwhile, the British backed a non-communist group, the 'London Poles'. Tension continued.

Now try this

List **three** areas of possible tension between East and West as a result of the division of Germany and the settling of borders at the Potsdam Conference.

Soviet expansion

By 1946, Albania, Bulgaria and Yugoslavia had communist governments. Between 1947 and 1949, the USSR spread its sphere of influence in Eastern Europe to nearby countries. Countries like Poland and Hungary became 'satellite states' under the control of the USSR.

How did Stalin take control?

- At Yalta and Potsdam, the USSR agreed to free elections in the countries in its sphere of influence.

- By the end of the war, the Soviet Red Army was in control of much of Eastern Europe. This encouraged communist parties across the region. The USSR made sure that local communist parties were loyal to Stalin.

- Stalin thought people would choose communism in free elections, however most did not. The USSR therefore fixed elections, making sure communists won.

  Fixing elections and then shutting down opposition parties was known as 'salami tactics'.

- Once in power, the communists shut down opposition parties and each country became a single-party state. Force and spreading fear silenced opposition.

- The USA saw this as a betrayal of the Yalta agreement. Others saw it as evidence of Soviet expansion into Europe.

- The USSR argued it needed to control Eastern Europe as a buffer zone, protecting itself from attack from the West.

Land taken by USSR at the end of WWII
Soviet-controlled communist countries
Non Soviet-controlled communist countries

The Soviet 'Iron Curtain': expansion in Europe, 1945–48.

For more on Yugoslavia, turn to page 8.

Growing Soviet influence in Eastern Europe: the 'Iron Curtain'

Country	How it became communist
Bulgaria	A communist government was elected in 1946, and all elected non-communists were executed.
Albania and Yugoslavia	Both states deposed (removed) their monarchies and established communist governments independent of the USSR, in the years 1945–46.
Romania	A communist-led coalition took power. However, by 1947, the communists had taken over and Romania became a one-party state.
Poland	At Yalta, Stalin promised to set up a joint communist/non-communist government. He then invited 16 non-communist leaders to Moscow and arrested them. Thousands of non-communists were arrested. The communists then 'won' the 1947 election.
Hungary	The communists lost the 1945 election, but the communist leader, Rákosi, took control of the secret police, executed and imprisoned his opponents. By 1948, he had turned Hungary into a communist state.
Czechoslovakia	Edvard Beneš set up a coalition government. However, the communists retained control of the army, the radio and the secret police. In 1948, they seized power, turning the country into a communist state.
East Germany	The original Soviet zone of occupation in Germany, it became a communist state in October 1949.

Now try this

Write a paragraph to describe how Stalin was able to gain control of Eastern Europe between 1945 and 1949.

US policies

In response to Soviet expansion, the USA increased its own involvement in Europe. Truman was determined to stop the spread of communist ideas and influence: a policy of **containment**. The purpose of the Truman Doctrine and the Marshall Plan was to contain communism.

Why did the USA change its policy?

- Europe was devastated after the war.
- In many countries people had no money, no jobs and were feeling hopeless.
- Communism was attractive to these people, especially in France and Italy: it made sure everyone had enough.
- Many in Eastern Europe had been liberated from Nazi rule by the Soviets.
- Countries like Poland, Romania and Bulgaria had already had communist governments forced on them and Truman feared this could happen in other countries too.
- Some governments (such as Greece and Turkey) were too poor to combat communist revolutions in their own countries. Greece was already experiencing civil war between Greek communists and the government.
- If Greece and Turkey became communist, then other countries across Europe and the Middle East would follow. This was known as the **Domino Theory**.

Post-war Berlin. Much of Europe had been destroyed during the war. Many people were homeless and starving. Truman feared that this could lead to people electing communist governments.

The Truman Doctrine was all about stopping the spread of communism. The USA was prepared to use both military and economic methods to prevent this spread.

The Truman Doctrine, 1947

In a speech in 1947, US President Truman set out why the USA should get involved:

- ✓ Countries faced a choice between either capitalism or communism.
- ✓ Communism was bad because it meant people could not be free. The USA must try to contain (hold back) this spread of communism.
- ✓ The USA should provide money and troops (if necessary) to help free governments to combat communist takeovers.

See page 8 for the Soviet reaction to the Truman Doctrine and Marshall Plan.

The Marshall Plan, 1947

- ✓ $13 billion of aid from the USA to help rebuild, stabilise and unify Europe.
- ✓ Communism appealed most to people with nothing to lose, so the Marshall Plan hoped to stop communism by making the capitalist system provide for the people.
- ✓ Countries must trade with the USA to get the money, boosting the US economy.
- ✓ 16 Western European countries took the money, including Britain, France and West Germany.
- ✓ The USSR criticised the Marshall Plan as an attack on them because it threatened communist control in Eastern Europe.

Now try this

In **two** sentences, explain why the USA hoped that the Marshall Plan would stop the spread of communism in Europe.

Stalin's reaction

The USSR was determined to defend itself from US threats, including the Marshall Plan. To counter US policy, Stalin reacted by announcing the formation of **Cominform** and **Comecon**.

Cominform

Cominform stood for the Communist Information Bureau. Stalin set it up in 1947. The bureau organised all the communist parties in Europe and their leadership so they would do what Moscow told them to.

Key points:

- ✓ Cominform got rid of any opposition to the USSR's control in satellite states.
- ✓ It encouraged communist parties in Western countries to block Marshall Plan assistance.

Dollar imperialism means using money to control other countries.

Comecon

Comecon stood for the Council for Mutual Economic Assistance. Stalin set it up in 1949. It was the USSR's alternative to the **dollar imperialism** of the Marshall Plan.

Key points:

- ✓ It built up trade links between Comecon countries.
- ✓ It also prevented Comecon countries signing up to the Marshall Plan.
- ✓ Comecon included the USSR, Bulgaria, Czechoslovakia, Hungary, Poland, Romania, Albania and, from 1950, the GDR (East Germany).

Consequences: the Iron Curtain

Western Europe was now in one camp. It was linked to the USA through the Marshall Plan and the US policy of containment of communism.

Eastern Europe was now in one camp: the 'Eastern bloc'. It was tied to the USSR as satellite states and the USSR believed socialist revolution would spread worldwide.

Europe was now divided into two spheres of influence: Western Europe (capitalist and pro-USA) and Eastern Europe (communist and controlled by the USSR). The line that divided these two spheres of influence was known as the Iron Curtain. Almost no contact, trade or tourism crossed that line.

For more about Churchill's 'Iron Curtain' speech, see page 4.

Yugoslavia

Yugoslavia had a unique relationship with the USSR.

- ✓ It was not liberated by the Red Army.
- ✓ Instead, a communist uprising had taken control, under Marshal Tito, in 1945, so Tito had no particular ties to Stalin.

Tito repeatedly ignored Stalin's wishes and kept his independence. In 1948, he openly fell out with Stalin, despite continuing to support communist ideology.

Tito's approach to the USA for Marshall Plan aid was a direct challenge to Stalin, who expelled Yugoslavia from Cominform. Yugoslavia became the only communist state in Europe outside the Iron Curtain.

Josep Broz Tito, shown here in 1945. The aid offered by the Marshall Plan created a huge contrast between Western countries, who were able to rebuild, and those in the Eastern bloc, who had very little. Stalin reacted with anger when Yugoslavia was tempted by the benefits of the aid.

Now try this

Look back at pages 6 and 7 to help with this question if you need to.

Write a paragraph to explain how Stalin reacted when Yugoslavia approached the USA for Marshall Plan aid, and why.

The Berlin Blockade

The USSR felt threatened by the rebuilding of Western Germany and West Berlin, and tensions increased further. This caused the Soviets to attempt to **blockade** (stop supplies getting into) West Berlin in June 1948.

For more information on the division of Germany, see page 5.

Causes, events and outcomes

Cause: Reunification

The USA wanted a united, capitalist Germany that it could trade with and that would help prevent the spread of communism.

Cause: Division

The USSR wanted Germany to be weak, communist and divided, so that it would never be able to attack the USSR again.

Cause: Bizonia and Western Germany

- The British and US zones joined together, to be easier to administer. The area was called Bizonia and was included in the Marshall Plan. Later, the French zone was added to create 'West Germany'.
- This was **not** popular with the USSR, as Stalin was not consulted. He thought Bizonia went against the agreements made at the Potsdam Conference, and he suspected the USA was aiming to permanently divide richer Western Germany from poorer Eastern Germany.
- The introduction of a new currency throughout the Western zone further angered Stalin.

Events: The Berlin Blockade

- The USSR had 1.5 million troops in its zone, whereas the Western countries had sent most of their troops home.
- Eastern Germany grew almost all the food that West Berlin ate.
- Berlin was deep in Soviet-controlled Germany, and divided into US, British, French and Soviet zones.
- In June 1948, the USSR closed all road, rail and canal links into West Berlin to force British, French and US troops to leave their zone in the city.
- The USSR blocked all supplies into Berlin to show it had the power to stop a divided Germany working.

Events: The Berlin Airlift

West Berlin couldn't last for many days without supplies. It looked like the Western powers would have to pull out of Berlin. That would look weak, undermining the USA's image in particular. So Western powers responded with an airlift – between 26 June 1948 and 30 September 1949, thousands of tonnes of supplies were flown into Berlin daily.

Outcome: West Germany

- Propaganda: The Berlin Airlift made the USA appear peaceful and generous.
- In September 1949, West Germany (FRG) was officially formed, with US support.
- In April 1949, Western European countries and the USA formed **NATO** to counter the Soviet military threat.

Outcome: East Germany

- Propaganda: The Blockade made the USSR appear aggressive and threatening.
- In October 1949, East Germany (GDR) was officially formed as a Soviet state.
- In May 1955, the USSR formed the **Warsaw Pact** to counter the military threat from NATO.

The Berlin Airlift was a **propaganda** victory for the West: showing the USSR to be the bully and the USA to be peaceful and supportive – not what Stalin had wanted.

For more on NATO and the Warsaw Pact, see page 15.

Now try this

Why did the USSR blockade West Berlin? List **three** reasons.

Revolution in China

In 1949, Mao Tse-tung's Chinese Communist Party (CCP) took control of China, ending the civil war that had raged there since 1945. This was significant for superpower relations as China's huge resources boosted the communist East and threatened to spread communism across Asia.

The Chinese Civil War: key events

1 The **USA** supports the Chinese government (GMD) against Japanese invaders during the Second World War, and continues to support the 'official' GMD government against the CCP from 1945.

2 The **USSR** invades Manchuria (north-east China) in August 1945 to defeat Japanese forces there.

3 The **USA** flies GMD troops into Manchuria in November 1945 to take over from the Soviets.

4 The **CCP**, boosted by aid from the Soviets, is in control of Manchuria by November 1948. Using the rich resources in Manchuria (and weapons left behind by the Japanese), and with widespread peasant support, they defeat the GMD by January 1949.

5 The People's Republic of China (PRC) is declared in October 1949.

Impact: China and the West

The West was alarmed at the CCP's triumph: the highest-populated country in the world had fallen under communist rule.

This was seen as a failure of Truman's policy of containment. To stop the spread of communism to more Asian countries, the West poured millions of dollars into nearby Taiwan and Japan.

Western countries refused to acknowledge the CCP as China's official government, and continued to back the exiled GMD leader, Chiang Kai-shek.

September 1950: the USA issued **National Security Council Resolution 68** to its military and security services. This increased military spending and strengthened its determination to fight against communism: the USA was ready for war to stop it spreading further.

Impact: China and the East

Although the USA saw the CCP's triumph as a win for Stalin, China was never truly part of the Soviet sphere.

The USSR was the only major country to recognise the PRC in 1949. Mao looked to Stalin to help develop China and protect it from US influences. The two countries signed a **Treaty of Friendship** in February 1950.

However, Stalin and Mao did not always agree. The Russian Revolution was led by urban (city) workers, but China was largely a country of rural peasants. Mao needed to find an ideology that worked for China. The USSR did not want its leadership challenged.

Relations between China and the USSR quickly got worse following Stalin's death in March 1953. Mao did not get on with Stalin's successor, Khrushchev, who was critical of Stalin.

Mao Tse-tung (1893–1976)

- A founding member of the CCP.
- His **guerrilla** tactics and ideology helped him become the unchallenged leader.
- Maoism – Chinese communism – became popular across Asia and the 'cult of Mao' made Mao worshipped in China.
- His rule of China led to a huge amount of violence and suffering, and also the 'great famine' (1958–62) in which millions died of starvation.

The Treaty of Friendship, 1950

- The Soviets promised $300 million of aid to China, but the interest rates were high and it had to be spent mainly on Soviet products.
- They accepted 8000 Chinese students to study science and technology in the USSR.
- They sent 20000 'experts' to assist in China's development, at China's cost.
- China had to surrender two major ports and mining rights to the Soviets.

Now try this

Write a paragraph to explain the significance of the CCP's victory in China for tensions between East and West.

The Korean War, 1950–53

During the Second World War, the Japanese invaded Korea. When the war ended, Korea was divided into two: the communist (Soviet-occupied) North and the capitalist (US-occupied) South. By 1950, the two countries were at war – involving both superpowers.

Events of the war

- In 1948, North and South Korea were officially established – North Korea led by Kim Il-Sung and South Korea by Syngman Rhee. Both leaders hoped to reunite Korea.
- In March 1949, Kim asked the USSR to help him invade the South. Stalin did not want to directly engage the US forces who were present in South Korea, so he encouraged China to support Kim instead.
- As soon as Kim invaded South Korea, the USA asked the UN to call a **ceasefire**. The UN demanded that Kim's forces withdraw. (The Soviets were **boycotting** – refusing to take part in – the UN at the time so could not vote against the ceasefire.)
- UN forces led by the USA were sent to support Rhee. The war became a stalemate.

Kim Il-Sung was a Soviet-trained politician, who had lived in the USSR and fought in the Soviet army. He was determined to spread communism to South Korea.

The military campaign

Timeline

Sept 1948 Kim Il-Sung forms communist Democratic People's Republic (North Korea).

June 1950 North Korea invades South Korea; UN call for ceasefire ignored.

Oct 1950 US-led UN forces enter North Korea and take capital, as USA shifts focus from containment to the defeat of communism.

April 1951 US General MacArthur sacked for calling for use of nuclear weapons.

July 1953 Ceasefire agreed.

July 1948 Syngman Rhee elected as president of capitalist Republic of (South) Korea.

Feb 1950 Soviets agree to supply military equipment to North Korea.

Sept 1950 US-led UN forces drive North Korea back to border (38th parallel, a line of latitude).

Oct–Nov 1950 China joins North Korea in a counterattack, capturing capital of South Korea.

June 1951 Peace negotiations start as war becomes a stalemate along the 38th parallel.

Significance for superpower relations

With UN backing, the USA could claim support from the international community. Their actions also demonstrated the USA's commitment to containing communism. US influence in the UN was clear.

This was the first time that US forces had fought an enemy largely equipped by the USSR. However, when US General MacArthur called for the use of nuclear weapons, he was dismissed.

It was clear that neither the USSR nor the USA wanted to risk a direct or full military struggle with their rival superpower. Instead, they could fight through other countries' wars.

The July 1953 ceasefire ended the war and restored the borders to almost exactly where they had been in 1950. On the surface, little had changed. The tensions continued.

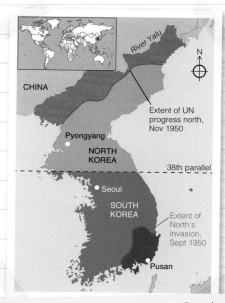

Division of Korea as agreed at the Potsdam Conference, 1945.

Now try this

1 Construct a flowchart to show how the division of Korea became an international crisis.
2 State the key outcome of the Korean War for Soviet–US relations.

The Vietnam War, 1955–75

The French colony of Vietnam was also occupied by the Japanese during the Second World War. Rather than welcoming back the French, Vietnamese communists continued to fight for their freedom. They were backed by the USSR and China, in order to spread communism further.

Military campaign against the French

After Japan's surrender, in September 1945 the Viet Minh independence fighters declared the establishment of the communist Democratic Republic of Vietnam. By 1952, the French had suffered 90,000 casualties trying to regain their control of the country.

In 1954, the French were defeated at Dien Bien Phu and decided to withdraw. The USA had paid for two-thirds of the French campaign in order to contain the spread of communism (and to counter Soviet and Chinese support for the Viet Minh). They were not prepared to abandon Vietnam.

At Geneva in July 1954, the world powers agreed to divide Vietnam into a communist North (under the Viet Minh) and a French South. It was to be reunited in elections two years later. The USA refused to sign.

Impact on relations: Domino Theory

US President Eisenhower was worried that, if Vietnam turned communist, it would lead to other nearby countries becoming communist too: like dominoes. Containment therefore became even more important.

Eisenhower was reluctant to commit to a military campaign. However, his 'New Look' policy led to increased US investment in South Vietnam: money, equipment and experts were all sent over to help contain communism.

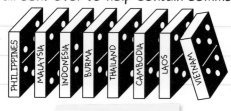

The 'domino' effect

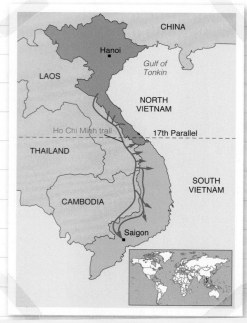

Vietnam and the Geneva division, also showing the Ho Chi Minh trail (named after the Viet Minh leader of North Korea).

Military campaign against the USA

South Vietnam was led by Ngo Dinh Diem. He was very anti-communist, but also corrupt and unpopular. The USA was determined to support him to counter communism.

From December 1960, the **Vietcong** formed – their aim was to overthrow Diem. They used the Ho Chi Minh Trail to build up forces in South Vietnam.

US President Kennedy increased US support to the South. Diem's increasing brutality led to his removal by US-backed rebels in 1963. After Kennedy's assassination in November, his successor, Lyndon Johnson, ordered full-scale US military involvement in 1965: 'Operation Rolling Thunder'. An eight-week campaign turned into a bloody three-year conflict. US forces struggled to engage successfully against the **guerrilla** forces of the local Vietcong in the unfamiliar jungle terrain. By 1972, the war still raged on as US forces gradually left Vietnam.

For more on the impact of this conflict on East–West relations, see pages 26 and 27.

Now try this

1 Construct a flowchart to show how the division of Vietnam became an international crisis.

2 In a short paragraph, explain the significance of the 'Domino Theory' for East–West relations.

The arms race

In 1945, the USA's latest weapon, the atom bomb, gave them a clear advantage over the USSR. However, the USSR developed their own nuclear weapon in 1949. After this, the two superpowers raced to stay ahead of each other by building bigger and more powerful weapons.

Timeline

The nuclear arms race

1945 USA drops two atom bombs on Japanese cities.

1949 USSR tests its first atom bomb.

1952 USA develops H-bomb (hydrogen bomb).

1953 USSR develops H-bomb.

See page 4 for more on the introduction of the atom bomb.

The significance of the nuclear arms race

The threat of the bomb loomed over East–West tensions after 1949.

Up to 1949, the USA thought it could use its advantage in nuclear weapons to discourage Soviet attack.

US military figures, such as General Curtis LeMay and General Douglas MacArthur, decided that the best strategy in the event of war with the USSR was to use nuclear weapons.

However, by the mid-1950s, nuclear weapons had been developed to include bigger warheads and missile delivery systems. This meant that any nuclear war would destroy both sides – resulting in **Mutually Assured Destruction (MAD)**.

This meant any military confrontation between both sides could rapidly escalate to nuclear war and world destruction.

The USA and the USSR had to find ways of stopping disputes between them turning into dangerous wars that involved nuclear weapons.

In 1961, the largest bomb the world had ever seen was tested by the USSR. It was more powerful than all the explosives from the Second World War combined!

Brinkmanship

During the Cold War there were several crises of **brinkmanship** (pushing events to the brink – edge – of conflict). After 1949, these crises between the superpowers led to a real fear of nuclear war and mutual destruction.

- In 1948, Stalin hoped his Berlin Blockade would not risk pushing the USA into using their nuclear weapons.

- In 1951, US President Truman sacked General MacArthur for repeatedly calling for nuclear weapons to be used against North Korea. Truman knew that the Soviets might retaliate if he did.

For more on General MacArthur, see the Korean War on page 11. For more on the Berlin Blockade, see page 9.

Effects of the arms race on ordinary people

The threat of nuclear war dramatically heightened Cold War tensions and impacted upon ordinary people as well as governments, for example:

- Defence costs increased for both sides to fuel the arms race, as the USA feared that they were falling behind the USSR.

- In the 1950s, 'duck and cover' campaigns taught attack response drill in the USA.

- In Britain in the 1970s, 'protect and survive' booklets were issued to citizens.

Now try this

The arms race between the superpowers affected the Cold War. List **three** impacts of the arms race on the Cold War.

The space race

The Cold War was driven by military and political rivalry, and this led to rapid advances in science and technology. Space exploration was a key battleground in the propaganda war, as both sides wanted to be seen to be leading the world by example.

Reasons for the space race

- **Propaganda:** both countries wished to demonstrate that their country and ideology was better than the other's.
- **Military rivalry:** there were military benefits to developing technology. The rockets developed could also be used to fire nuclear weapons, widening the reach of Cold War conflict.

Intercontinental ballistic missiles (ICBMs) could be carried thousands of miles: distance was not a safeguard against attack. The **Polaris** missile was developed by the USA to be fired from a submarine, providing a secret and mobile launch platform.

Soviet propaganda poster showing a worker and an engineer during the space race.

Race to be first

The successful launch of the **Sputnik** satellite in 1957 was a massive victory for the Soviets. For the first time, the communists had a technological advantage over the capitalists. This was confirmed when the Soviets put **Yuri Gagarin** into space.

However, US President Kennedy was determined that the race was not over. He promised to put a man on the moon by the end of the 1960s. In 1969, millions across the world watched Neil Armstrong walk on the moon – the triumph of the USA.

Superpower rivalry led to one of mankind's greatest achievements, and space exploration was a key theme of the Cold War throughout the 1970s.

Timeline

Oct 1957 USSR: Sputnik is first manmade satellite to orbit the Earth.

Dec 1958 USA: SCORE is first communications satellite, launched by the Atlas rocket.

Nov 1957 USSR: Laika, a dog, is first animal in orbit.

Apr 1961 USSR: Yuri Gagarin is first person in space.

May 1961 USA: Alan Shepard pilots first successful space flight.

June 1963 USSR: Valentina Tereshkova is first woman in space.

July 1969 USA: Neil Armstrong is first person on the moon.

April 1971 USSR: Salyut 1 is first crewed space station.

Apollo space programme

Launched in 1961, the US **Apollo** space programme was dedicated to space exploration. It achieved its first manned flight in 1968, before landing Armstrong on the moon in 1969. It wasn't until July 1975 that the first joint Soviet–US space mission was launched: the Apollo–Soyuz mission. It symbolised a changing relationship and the thawing of the Cold War.

Now try this

List **two** impacts of the space race on the Cold War.

NATO and the Warsaw Pact

After Stalin announced **Comecon** in January 1949, **NATO** was set up in April by the West. The Soviets saw NATO as a threat and, in 1955, formed the **Warsaw Pact**. This increased Cold War tensions in Europe even further. Both sides were now geared up for a possible war.

For more on Comecon, see page 8.

NATO: membership and purpose

✓ The North Atlantic Treaty Organisation (NATO) was a military alliance made up of the USA, Britain, Canada, Italy, Belgium, France, the Netherlands, Portugal, Luxembourg, Iceland, Denmark and Norway. West Germany joined in 1955.

✓ NATO was based around the principle of **collective security** (if one member country was attacked, the others had to assist it).

✓ NATO was directed against a possible military attack from the USSR on Western Europe. The USA was now committed to defending Europe from communism.

Impact of NATO on East–West rivalry

- After the Berlin Blockade and the USSR's development of an atom bomb, the USA and Western Europe were not prepared to accept future Soviet aggression.

- Stalin saw NATO as an act of aggression aimed at the USSR. The USSR therefore began to strengthen its control over Eastern Europe. This resulted in the formation of the Warsaw Pact in 1955.

- The USA promised funds to improve the military forces of its allies, and set up US bases and troops in NATO countries – a direct threat to the USSR.

Warsaw Pact: membership and purpose

✓ The Warsaw Pact was a collective defence treaty involving the USSR, Poland, Hungary, East Germany, Czechoslovakia, Romania, Albania and Bulgaria.

✓ It was set up on 14 May 1955 following West Germany's entry into NATO.

Stalin died in 1953. His successor, Nikita Khrushchev, launched a process of 'de-Stalinisation' in the USSR from 1956. This destabilised the Warsaw Pact countries.

Impact of the Warsaw Pact

- The formation of the Warsaw Pact meant there were now two opposing alliances in Europe separated by the Iron Curtain.

- Both alliances planned for military action against the other, including the use of nuclear and conventional weapons.

- The Warsaw Pact gave the USSR direct control over the armed forces of its satellite states, thus strengthening its grip on Eastern Europe.

- These military rivalries just needed a spark to ignite into a possible global war.

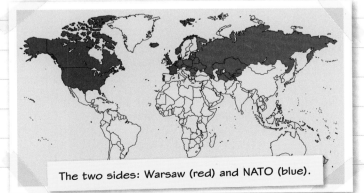

The two sides: Warsaw (red) and NATO (blue).

The opposing forces in Europe

NATO: 50 army divisions, US nuclear weapons (plus Britain from 1952, France from 1960).

Warsaw: 175 army divisions, Soviet nuclear weapons (plus 35,000 tanks, 10,000 aircraft).

Now try this

In one sentence, summarise the impact of NATO on the Cold War.

Hungary: protest and reform

Stalin's successor, Khrushchev, suggested that Soviet policy might **thaw** towards more **'peaceful co-existence'**: a policy of **de-Stalinisation**. This destabilised the Warsaw countries and raised hopes of increased independence. Hungary was the first country to see those hopes crushed.

Impact of Soviet rule

Hungary and its people suffered a lot under Stalin's control.

- Food and industrial products were shipped off to the USSR.

- Any opposition in Hungary was ruthlessly wiped out. By the early 1950s, up to 5% of the population was imprisoned.

- Mátyás Rákosi was a brutal ruler. He called himself 'Stalin's best pupil', but was known as the 'Bald Butcher'.

- Communist rule became very unpopular.

- Soviet troops were permanently stationed in Hungary and dealt with any opposition quickly.

> A **thaw** here means a lowering of hostilities and tensions. '**Peaceful co-existence**' means living together in peace, without fighting.

The Hungarian uprising in 1956, showing a statue of Stalin that has been pulled down.

The protest movement

When Stalin died, Khrushchev took over as Soviet leader. In 1956, in his 'secret speech', Khrushchev hinted that Soviet control would relax: a policy of de-Stalinisation.

In October 1956, poor harvests and bread shortages meant that Hungarians started demonstrating against communist control. Statues of Stalin were pulled down and local communists were attacked. Khrushchev appointed a more liberal prime minister for Hungary – Imre Nagy – in the hope that the situation would calm down.

> De-Stalinisation meant that the USSR no longer saw itself as a dictatorship. Instead it became a one-party state, governed by the Politburo, with Khrushchev as its leader. This gave rise to hopes that Soviet repression and control might thaw and East Europeans might live in peace beside the USSR.
>
> Many Hungarians mistakenly believed that the end of Stalin's rule would bring an end to communism in Hungary. Soviet troops had already withdrawn from neighbouring Austria in 1955 and protests in Poland had already led to some limited reforms.

The reforms of Nagy

Nagy wanted these reforms for Hungary:

- Leave the Warsaw Pact and become a neutral country.

- Hold free elections leading to no more communist government.

- UN protection from the USSR.

> However, this was a problem for the USSR because if Nagy succeeded in Hungary other countries in Eastern Europe would follow. The Warsaw Pact would collapse. 'Peaceful co-existence' could mean the end of the Eastern bloc, so Soviet fears about this led to a return to harsher policies.

 Now try this

Write a paragraph to explain why many Hungarians were prepared to protest against the communist government in October 1956.

Soviet reaction

Khrushchev disapproved of Nagy's reforms and in 1956 Soviet troops invaded Hungary. This provoked a strong reaction in the West. Many countries condemned the invasion.

Soviet fears

- Khrushchev didn't like Nagy's reforms and proposals. The Soviets feared that, if Hungary left the Warsaw Pact, other countries would soon follow.

- Khrushchev feared that Nagy's actions threatened communist rule. He claimed communists were being slaughtered in Hungary. This may have been propaganda, but was based on truth.

- Hungarian communists had been killed and members of the state security forces (the AVH) had been attacked in the violence of October 1956. Khrushchev feared the unrest would spread to other satellite states.

Soviet reaction

On 4 November 1956, Khrushchev sent 200 000 Soviet troops into Hungary to depose Nagy and restore order.

Damage in Budapest caused by Soviet troops during the invasion of Hungary, 4 November 1956.

The consequences of the Soviet invasion of Hungary

1 At least 4000 Hungarians were killed, and around 1000 Soviet troops. Many Hungarian soldiers loyal to Nagy and the revolution fought against Soviet troops. As many as 200 000 refugees fled across the borders.

2 Nagy and his government were deposed. Nagy was arrested, tried and executed. Khrushchev wanted to prevent rebellions in other communist countries, such as Poland, and hoped he could do so by making an example of Nagy.

3 A new leader, János Kádár, was appointed. He introduced the Fifteen Point Programme, which aimed to re-establish communist rule in Hungary. Kádár's policies were more moderate than those of other Soviet satellite states and resulted in Hungary having better living standards than other East-European states. Hungarians, aware that the USA was not prepared to help them, grudgingly accepted this modified form of communist rule.

International reaction and the effects on the Cold War

The United Nations condemned Soviet actions. Some countries boycotted the 1956 Olympics in protest. But stronger actions did not happen.

↓

The USA supported Hungary's uprising – with money, medical aid and words. The USA accepted 80 000 refugees from Hungary.

↓

But the USA couldn't send troops: it would risk nuclear war with the USSR.

↓

Hungary was on its own against the USSR: it had to give in.

↓

Satellite states saw that the USA would not defend them against the USSR. Soviet control retightened across Eastern Europe as it was clear the USA would not interfere.

The invasion highlighted the differences between East and West, and made the limits of Khrushchev's 'peaceful co-existence' clear. It also showed that the USA would not risk war to interfere in the Soviet sphere of influence.

Now try this

Summarise the following (in no more than 100 characters each): a) Khrushchev's fears and reasons for invading Hungary; b) what the international reaction showed to the USSR.

U2 Crisis and peace process

As a result of increased tensions between the superpowers, Khrushchev issued the Berlin Ultimatum. This demanded the removal of all Western troops from Berlin and triggered a series of summits (talks). The atmosphere of espionage (spying) and mistrust almost led to disaster.

Tensions between East and West

West Berlin

- West Berlin was inside the Soviet-controlled East.
- Divided Berlin gave the USA a foothold inside the Soviet Eastern bloc.
- Some Germans in East Germany did not like having a communist government. There were also better jobs with higher wages in the West.
- It was easy to get to West Germany from the western zones in Berlin.

The refugee problem in Berlin

- Between 1949 and 1961, 2.7 million East Germans crossed from the East to the West in Berlin. The population of West Germany increased while the economy benefitted from an influx of skilled workers.
- Many skilled workers left for the West, leaving the East with a skills shortage.
- This looked bad for the Soviets: people clearly preferred West Germany to East Germany.

Khrushchev's Berlin Ultimatum, November 1958

- All Berlin belonged to East Germany and occupying troops must leave within six months.
- The USSR knew that, if it tried to push the West out of Berlin by force, it would start a war that the USSR could not win, as the USA had more nuclear weapons.

The Paris Peace Summit and the peace process

Summit	Outcome
Geneva (May 1959), involving foreign representatives only	No solution agreed but a further summit organised for Camp David in the USA.
Camp David (Sept 1959), involving Eisenhower and Khrushchev	No solution agreed but a further meeting arranged in Paris.
Paris Summit (May 1960), involving Eisenhower and Khrushchev	A disaster. Khrushchev stormed out after the USA failed to apologise for having a US spy plane over the USSR.
Vienna Conference (June 1961), involving Kennedy and Khrushchev	Neither was willing to back down. Khrushchev saw Kennedy's youth and inexperience as a weakness to exploit.

Atmosphere of mistrust

Both superpowers used spies. In the 1950s and 1960s, the USA feared communism (the second 'Red Scare') and communist spies.

- The **House Un-American Activities Committee (HUAC)** was set up in 1938 to investigate possible communist activity.
- In 1950, State Department official Alger Hiss was found guilty of passing on secrets to the USSR.
- Julius and Ethel Rosenberg were executed for passing on nuclear secrets.
- Senator McCarthy's 'witch-hunt' became known as 'McCarthyism'. It was often based on totally untrue allegations.

The U2 Crisis and its effects

The USA used U2 spy planes for information gathering, photographing the USSR from the air. The Soviets knew about this.

On 1 May 1960, US pilot Gary Powers was shot down and captured. The USA denied it was a spy plane, but the Soviets had clear evidence. Knowing the USSR also had spies, Eisenhower refused to say sorry or say it would not happen again.

Khrushchev stormed out of the **Paris Peace Summit**, after only one day. A final summit was held in Vienna in 1961. Khrushchev reissued his ultimatum.

Now try this

Tensions were now higher than before summits. Some think that Khrushchev used the crisis to look strong and did not want the talks to succeed.

In no more than 140 characters, explain why the U2 Crisis was important.

Reasons for the Berlin Wall

The USSR and the USA started negotiations to sort out the problem of the division of Berlin, but the summit meetings broke down following the U2 Crisis. Khrushchev's response was to order the building of the Berlin Wall in 1961.

For more on the problem of Berlin and the U2 Crisis, see page 18.

Why did the Soviet government construct the Berlin wall?

Khrushchev had thought he could take advantage of Kennedy's inexperience by issuing the Berlin Ultimatum in 1958.

For more on the Berlin Ultimatum, see page 18.

⬇

The four summit meetings of 1959–61 had failed to resolve the problem in Berlin, and President Kennedy started to prepare the USA for nuclear war.

⬇

Khrushchev wanted to look strong but could not risk a nuclear war with the USA.

⬇

Western powers stayed in Berlin: West Berlin remained a symbol of Western prosperity.

⬇

The refugee problem continued: thousands of East Germans **defected** every day in early 1961, using the Berlin border to reach West Germany.

Defected means abandoned their country (in this case for the West).

⬇

Khrushchev's response was to build the Berlin Wall, which began in August 1961 and prevented East Berliners from leaving West Berlin.

Building the Berlin Wall

- On 12 August 1961, East German troops erected a barbed wire fence around the city and between East and West Berlin.
- Over the next three months, the fence became a heavily guarded concrete wall. Soviet tanks were deployed to stop Western access to the East.
- By the end of October 1961, West Berlin was completely cut off from East Germany.

Do not confuse the construction of the Berlin Wall with the Berlin Blockade. You can revise the Berlin Blockade on page 9.

Building the Berlin Wall, August 1961. Note the number of soldiers in the background. Over 200 East Germans were shot trying to cross the wall between 1961 and 1989.

Now try this

Why did Khrushchev construct the Berlin Wall in August 1961? Write a short paragraph to explain your answer.

To answer this question, you will also need to refer back to the previous page.

Kennedy's response

The construction of the Berlin Wall in 1961 affected relations between the USSR and the USA, but it made war over Berlin less likely. The Cold War struggles now shifted away from Germany.

Impact of the Wall: Kennedy's response

- The USA made an official complaint to the USSR about the Wall. Kennedy needed to show he was strong enough to stand up to communism.

- Western (British, US and French) troops remained in Berlin.

- The number of military alerts in Berlin declined as a result of the Wall, easing tensions between the USA and USSR. As Kennedy commented, it was better than war. Focus shifted away from Germany.

- The Wall was an obvious barrier between the freedoms enjoyed by West Berliners and those denied to East Berliners. West Berlin became a lasting symbol of freedom.

- In June 1963, Kennedy made a speech in West Berlin to make clear his – and the USA's – commitment to fighting communism. The 'Thaw' was over.

Impact of the Wall: the USSR

- The Wall solved the refugee problem, as East Germans could no longer travel to West Germany. This halted the loss of skilled workers and its economic impact.

- It was a humiliation for the USSR and a propaganda victory for the West. It suggested that East Germans preferred living in capitalist West Germany and had to be forced to stay in the communist East.

- It showed that the Soviets had given up on unifying Berlin under communist rule, as Khrushchev had originally demanded in November 1958.

- Khrushchev thought that Kennedy had shown weakness by allowing the Wall to be built, and this encouraged him to think about deploying missiles in Cuba.

For more on the Cuban Missile Crisis, turn to page 22.

Kennedy's visit to West Berlin, 1963

- In Kennedy's famous visit to West Berlin, he claimed 'Ich bin ein Berliner' ('I am a Berliner [a citizen of Berlin]') and outlined the evils of communism.

- His speech was an expression of solidarity with the people of West Berlin. The fact that Kennedy chose to visit West Berlin personally and give this speech was significant – it demonstrated that the USA and NATO were prepared to defend West Berlin from communist attack.

- Kennedy was also speaking after the Cuban Missile Crisis had ended and was showing his audience – both German and American – that he was not 'soft on communism'.

Kennedy speaking in West Berlin, 26 June 1963. The USA made full use of the propaganda opportunities the Wall provided. The message to Khrushchev was clear.

The Iron Curtain divides East and West

The construction of the Berlin Wall filled the last remaining gap in the Iron Curtain and meant that Europe was now completely divided.

For Churchill's Iron Curtain speech, see page 4.

There were two Germanys.

The Iron Curtain divisions

There were two different ideologies (capitalism and communism).

There were two different alliances (NATO and the Warsaw Pact).

Now try this

Imagine you are a citizen of Berlin in 1963. In a short text message to a fellow Berliner, summarise the significance of Kennedy's Berlin speech of 26 June 1963 to West Berlin.

Castro's revolution

A revolution in Cuba in 1959 set it against its neighbour, the USA. The USA attempted to bring Cuba back into its sphere of influence. Instead, Cuba's leader Fidel Castro asked the USSR for help with defence. Suddenly, the Cold War was happening within 100 miles of the US mainland.

The Cuban Revolution: Castro's role

- The USA had helped Cuba to gain independence from Spain in 1898. US businesses invested heavily in Cuban land and industry.
- From 1933 to 1958, Batista's unpopular and corrupt government profited – and helped the US businesses to do likewise.
- Between 1956 and 1958, Castro led a revolution that toppled the government. The USA refused to talk to Castro.
- Castro seized the US-owned businesses for the state and set up a socialist government. He built economic links with the USSR, for example, trading Soviet oil for Cuban sugar. The relationship between Castro and the USA got worse.

Why did the revolution turn into a crisis?

- The USA refused to recognise Castro's government and banned all trade with Cuba. Cuba was now totally dependent on the USSR.
- The USA did not want a socialist country in its sphere of influence, especially not one with close links to the USSR.
- In January 1961, the USA broke off all diplomatic relations with Cuba.
- The CIA tried to assassinate Castro, but failed. They convinced President Kennedy that a US-backed invasion of Cuba, designed to overthrow Castro, could solve the problem.

Cuban President Fidel Castro pictured during a visit to the USA in 1959.

The Bay of Pigs incident, 17 April 1961

The Bay of Pigs incident was a failed military invasion of Cuba undertaken by a CIA-sponsored paramilitary group.

What the CIA told Kennedy:

👍 The invasion will look like a Cuban revolt – we've trained Cuban exiles and disguised old US planes as Cuban.

👍 Castro's control of Cuba is very weak.

👍 Most Cubans hate Castro. (In fact, most Cubans did not want Batista back again, because he had been corrupt.)

What actually happened:

👎 The planes were recognised as US planes and photographed: the world knew that the USA had backed the invasion.

👎 In fact, Castro knew of the invasion in advance and 1400 US-backed troops met 20 000 of Castro's troops. The US-backed troops surrendered.

Impact of the Bay of Pigs

- Kennedy was embarrassed, and looked weak and inexperienced.
- Castro could claim a great victory against the mighty USA.
- It ended all chances of a friendly USA–Cuba relationship.
- Castro announced that he was a communist.
- Cuba and the USSR started building closer ties – including military defence for Cuba.

Now try this

List **two** things that Castro did and **two** things that the USA did that led to a Cuban crisis.

The Cuban Missile Crisis

The Soviet response to the Cuban crisis was to build missile sites on Cuba to deter US attacks. When the USA discovered these missile sites, the crisis threatened to develop into nuclear war. The USA was torn on how best to respond: attack while it could or do everything to avoid war.

Developing crisis: Khrushchev's role

Khrushchev saw Cuba as a fix to a key Soviet strategic problem. The USA had missiles close to the USSR (for example, in Italy and Turkey), but the USSR had no missiles close to the USA.

Khrushchev thought Kennedy was weak and that he could successfully bully the US president. He was also keen to increase Soviet influence in nearby South America.

Castro saw Soviet missiles as a great way to prevent the USA from invading Cuba again. He had been driven to ask for Soviet aid by the USA's reaction to his revolution and their refusal to talk.

Kennedy looked weak to Khrushchev because he had not reacted to the building of the Berlin Wall and because of the failed Bay of Pigs incident, both in 1961. See pages 19 and 20 for more on the Wall, and page 21 for more on the Bay of Pigs.

Soviet missile launch site in Cuba

Kennedy's role and US fears

- When the US public learned that they were in range of Soviet missiles for the first time, there was panic. Kennedy had to act decisively – but did not want war.

- The USA could not allow a communist country so close to its borders a chance to spread communism into the Americas.

- Kennedy announced a blockade of Cuba: no ships from any country were allowed through. US ships were ordered to fire upon any ships that tried to pass through.

- The line had been drawn: US troops were put on DEFCON 3 – only two levels below the level for nuclear war. Protestors in the USA called for restraint.

Make sure you are clear about the chronology (order of events) of the Cuban Missile Crisis and how it fits into the timeline of the Cold War.

The 'Thirteen Days', 1962

Timeline

16 Oct Kennedy is informed that US spy planes have found missile sites on Cuba.

24 Oct USSR says a blockade is an act of aggression and its ships will ignore it.

27 Oct Khrushchev offers to remove missiles from Cuba if USA does so from Turkey. Robert Kennedy sets up a deal in which the USA would secretly withdraw warheads.

Sept Soviet ships carry nuclear warheads and missiles to Cuba.

20 Oct Kennedy decides against an attack. Orders a blockade of Cuba.

25 Oct USA and USSR prepare for immediate nuclear attack.

28 Oct Khrushchev agrees to the deal: missiles withdrawn; in return USA agrees never to attack Cuba, and pulls out of Turkey.

Now try this

Who was more to blame for the Cuban Missile Crisis – Khrushchev or Kennedy? Write a short statement explaining why Khrushchev was to blame. Then write a short statement explaining why Kennedy was to blame.

Results of the crisis

During the Cuban Missile Crisis, the world came very close to nuclear war. In order to avoid this happening again, steps were taken to improve relations between the USA and the USSR.

Short-term results of the crisis

- Communist Cuba survived as Kennedy gave assurances the USA would not invade again.
- The USSR publicly withdrew its missiles from Cuba, to promote world peace. The USA secretly withdrew its missiles from Turkey in response.
- The USSR looked weak, as the world did not know the USA had removed missiles from Turkey. This undermined Khrushchev and Brezhnev replaced him as Soviet leader in 1964.
- The US peace lobby gained influence, as their desire to avoid war resulted in the withdrawal of the US missiles.

The dangers of the crisis

Kennedy told his brother, Robert, that the US response was a gamble: it certainly was!

Castro's response: Castro ordered Soviet forces on Cuba to be ready to fight. On 23 October 1962, a Soviet fleet approached the blockade: it was a moment of brinkmanship, to see who would back down.

⬇

The brink of war: On 25 October, a Soviet ship approached Cuba and was met by the US Navy. As it was only an oil tanker, it was allowed through, despite refusing to cooperate. Kennedy did not want to provoke Khrushchev.

⬇

Invasion plans: On 26 October, over 120 000 US troops assembled to prepare for invading Cuba. The same day, a letter arrived from Khrushchev, offering to back down if the USA promised not to invade Cuba.

⬇

First shots: On 27 October, a US ship spotted a Soviet submarine close to Cuba. It fired depth charges to force the submarine to surface. The captain intended to fire back, but was overruled by a senior officer on board.

The same day, a US U2 spyplane was shot down above Cuba. Another plane entered Soviet airspace above Alaska and was fired at.

Khrushchev's second letter arrived shortly afterwards, offering the terms agreed.

Long-term results

The Cuban Missile Crisis showed how easily a nuclear war could start. On 27 October 1962, the Soviet submarine captain or the Cuban gunner could have sparked nuclear war. Instead, the crisis began a move towards **Détente** (an easing of tension) – and a more informed relationship between the USA and the USSR.

- The Hotline Agreement created a direct communication link between Washington and Moscow.
- The Limited Test Ban Treaty (August 1963) – both sides agreed to ban all nuclear weapon testing except underground tests.
- In 1963, Kennedy gave a speech about working with the USSR to focus on their 'common interests'.
- The USSR was determined to catch up with the USA in the arms race and achieved this by 1965. This meant Mutually Assured Destruction (MAD): war would be so terrible that it must be avoided at all costs.
- The USA and the USSR signed the Outer Space Treaty in 1967, which limited the deployment of nuclear weapons in space.
- They also signed the Nuclear Non-Proliferation Treaty in 1968, which prevented nuclear weapons being given to other countries.

Now try this

What was the main outcome of the Cuban Missile Crisis for the Cold War? Write a short paragraph to explain your answer.

Dubček and the Prague Spring

Like in Hungary, a relaxation of control in Czechoslovakia – a satellite state – led to a challenge to Soviet authority in 1968. The 'Prague Spring' movement was a threat to the Warsaw Pact.

For more on the satellite states, see page 17. For more on Hungary, see page 16.

The impact of Soviet rule

- Czechoslovakia's economy and living standards declined under the communist one-party state.
- Any opposition to communism was crushed and the press was controlled.
- Communist rule became very unpopular.
- In the mid-1960s, Czech economist Ota Šik called for economic reform. After his call was rejected, in 1966 he called for full political reform with popular support.

Dubček and the Prague Spring movement

✓ In January 1968, Alexander Dubček was made the Czechoslovakian leader.

 He was a good friend of Soviet leader Leonid Brezhnev, who believed Dubček could calm the calls for reform.

 Dubček was a communist and supporter of the Warsaw Pact, but wanted to make communism better and easier to live under. He called his programme 'socialism with a human face'.

Dubček's reforms

Dubček's reforms resulted in the 'Prague Spring' – a period of increased political freedom – from April 1968. Lots of criticism of communism followed.

- Press censorship ended, public meetings and freedom of speech were allowed.
- Other parties were allowed alongside the communists, increasing democracy.
- More power was given to the Czechoslovakian parliament and Soviet control was reduced.
- The economy was also reformed, with 'market socialism' allowing for the introduction of some 'capitalist elements'. State control was ended.
- The secret police were also restricted.

How Czechs responded to the reforms

Students, intellectuals, workers and young members of the Communist Party of Czechoslovakia welcomed Dubček's reforms enthusiastically.

As a result of the reforms, writers such as Václav Havel and Milan Kundera wrote books that were highly critical of Soviet-style communism.

Not all Czechs were happy: members of the secret police and some senior army officers lost power and status as a result of the reforms and they resented this.
The Prague Spring horrified many older Czech communists, as they felt it would lead to the collapse of communism in Czechoslovakia.

Immediate effect on Warsaw Pact countries

- Brezhnev and other communists in Eastern Europe, such as Erich Honecker, the leader of East Germany, were especially concerned. They feared the Prague Spring would lead to demands for reform elsewhere in the Eastern bloc that would threaten communist rule there.
- Polish students began calling for their own 'Dubček' in protests against their government. Support was also given from independent communist Yugoslavia and from Romania, a member of the Warsaw Pact.
- Brezhnev now had a dilemma: Dubček was a friend and military action would damage the USSR's reputation. On the other hand, if he did nothing, expectations of further reforms would rise and the whole Eastern bloc might collapse.

Now try this

In what ways was the Prague Spring a threat to the Warsaw Pact countries? List **two** reasons.

The USSR's response

Soviet leader Brezhnev could not accept Dubček's reforms so the USSR invaded Czechoslovakia in August 1968. Brezhnev established the Brezhnev Doctrine in order to defend the Warsaw Pact countries from any future security 'threats'.

USSR's response to Dubček's reforms

- Brezhnev could not allow the reforms, as any weakness in control could mean the break-up of the Warsaw Pact – even though this wasn't Dubček's intention.

- Brezhnev failed to convince Dubček to stop the reforms. He had to act, or risk looking weak – as his predecessor had over Cuba – and this could lead to his removal.

- In August 1968, the USSR sent tanks to Prague and Dubček was arrested.

- Czechoslovakia returned to being under strict Soviet control.

The Soviet invasion of Czechoslovakia, August 1968.

The Brezhnev Doctrine

In November 1968, Brezhnev made it clear that the USSR was determined to maintain communist governments in Europe and elsewhere – and would again use force if necessary to protect communism. This was known as the Brezhnev Doctrine.

| From now on, the USSR declared the right to invade any Eastern bloc country that was threatening the security of the Eastern bloc as a whole. | → | The USA condemned the invasion but did nothing to stop it: it feared war. | → | Western European communist parties were horrified and declared themselves independent from the Soviet Communist Party. | → | Yugoslavia and Romania also backed off from the USSR, which weakened the USSR's grip on Eastern Europe. |

Effect on the West

- The USA and West Germany condemned the invasion of Czechoslovakia and the Brezhnev Doctrine. Talks about improving relations ended.

- They offered no military support or assistance to the Czechs. What happened behind the Iron Curtain was for the Soviets alone to decide.

- The USA was already bogged down in the Vietnam War and also did not want to provoke an international crisis.

- Other communist leaders, such as those in France and Italy, were horrified by the invasion. France and Italy therefore began to end their links with the USSR.

- It did not damage the growing Détente between East and West as fewer than 100 Czechs died as a result of the invasion.

Effect on the East

- The invasion and the Brezhnev Doctrine limited reforms in other Warsaw Pact countries who feared a Soviet invasion.

- Countries such as Poland followed policies that ignored public opinion, which increasingly demanded change. This led to public protests.

- The invasion strengthened Soviet control over the Eastern bloc as they could use military force to ensure their dominance.

- Yet the crisis also exposed differences in the Eastern bloc. Both Romania and Yugoslavia condemned the invasion and signed alliances with communist China, dividing the communist world.

- There were protests in China and fear of Soviet interference there increased the division between China and the USSR.

Now try this

What impact did the Prague Spring have on superpower relations? List **two** impacts.

Sources of tension

Relations between the two superpowers improved towards the end of the 1960s. However, tensions continued because the ideologies and aims of the superpowers were still different. The nuclear threat also remained. So, the situation continued to be complicated.

Differing ideologies

See page 25 for the Brezhnev Doctrine and page 12 for the Domino Theory.

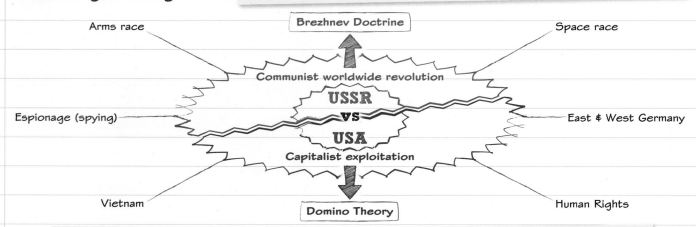

For more on the arms race and space race, see pages 13–14. It was important to both sides to be seen as 'winning' these races, so that their ideology was seen as strongest.

Spying formed part of the arms and space races and tensions over the division of Germany continued throughout the Cold War. For more on this, see pages 18 and 20.

Conflicting ideologies in Vietnam

The USA wanted to stop communism from spreading in Vietnam and neighbouring countries. Communists resented the USA forcing their capitalist ideology on those Vietnamese who were communist.

The war continued throughout the 1960s, at a cost of almost 60000 American lives. This made improving relations with the USSR difficult. The war became increasingly unpopular in the USA too.

The USA finally withdrew in 1973, leaving South Vietnam to fight alone. By 1975, the whole of Vietnam was communist.

Revise Vietnam on page 12, Hungary on page 16 and Czechoslovakia on page 24.

'Anti-Soviet agitation and propaganda' was the name of a criminal offence. It was often used against Soviet people who spoke out against Soviet ideology and, during the 1960s–1980s, could lead to imprisonment or exile.

Soviet record on human rights

Communism placed the state before the rights and freedoms of its people. Therefore, many in the West saw the Cold War as a fight for freedom against communist oppression.

- Many books remained illegal and state opponents faced exile in the **Gulag** prison camps of Siberia (or confinement in special 'hospitals').

- The invasions of Hungary (1956) and Czechoslovakia (1968) showed the world that the USSR was not worried about human rights.

Concerns over human rights remained a source of tension. However, preventing further conflict was a higher priority for the USA.

The **KGB** (Soviet secret police) had its powers limited in 1960, but was still able to deal with 'anti-Soviet agitation and propaganda'. In the mid-1970s, there were an estimated 10000 Soviet political prisoners.

Now try this

Explain how the following caused further tension between the superpowers: a) conflicting ideologies; b) human rights. Write **two** sentences for **each** explanation.

Détente and SALT 1

In the early 1970s, tensions between the USA and USSR began to relax. This easing of tension led to a period of closer cooperation, called **Détente**, and the SALT 1 Treaty, as both sides tried to restrict the chance of nuclear conflict.

The China–Soviet split: Relations between Mao's China and the USSR broke down under Khrushchev and Brezhnev. This made both countries more willing to cooperate with the USA, and the USA was happy to exploit this.

Mao became more critical of the Soviet bureaucrats and their loss of revolutionary spirit. He wanted to free China from its dependence on Soviet 'expertise'.

The arms race: The Cuban Missile Crisis marked the start of attempts to reduce tensions and avoid nuclear war. In 1963, the Partial Test Ban Treaty and the new 'hotline' between the USA and the USSR began the process. When the Chinese developed nuclear weapons in 1964, the concerns of the USA and the USSR grew. They hoped cooperation might reduce the risk of this technology spreading further.

Domestic: The arms and space races cost billions of dollars. The USSR faced bankruptcy if it continued spending. The USA faced social issues and protests at home against its international policies.

Reasons for Détente

Vietnam: The war showed that military dominance did not guarantee victory. Both the USA and the USSR started to rely more on indirect action rather than military intervention.

From the end of the 1960s, there was greater communication between the USA and the USSR. Tensions decreased between the two superpowers and they agreed to limit the number of nuclear weapons.

Strategic Arms Limitation Treaty (SALT), 1972

SALT 1 was the most serious attempt between the superpowers to limit nuclear weapons. US talks with China earlier that year encouraged the more isolated Soviets to cooperate.

- ✓ No further production of strategic ballistic weapons (short-range, lightweight missiles).
- ✓ No increase in number of intercontinental ballistic weapons (ICBMs) (though new ones could be added to replace old ones).
- ✓ No new nuclear missile launchers. New submarines that could launch nuclear weapons (SLBMs) only allowed to replace existing missile launchers.
- ✓ The Anti-Ballistic Missile (ABM) Treaty limited both sides to two ABM deployment areas.

The roles of Brezhnev and Nixon

From 1968, there were regular summit meetings between Brezhnev and Nixon. They were unlikely champions for peace, but they worked together surprisingly well. They played a key role in making SALT happen.

- ✓ Brezhnev had been in Stalin's Politburo and a key figure under Khrushchev.
- ✓ Nixon had been anti-communist all his life and was Eisenhower's vice president.
- ✓ Their experience helped them to make progress where younger leaders had failed. They knew what was at stake.
- ✓ They had both seen the darkest days of the Cold War. They found they had a surprising amount in common.
- ✓ Nixon made historic visits both to Moscow and to China during this time.

How effective was SALT 1?

SALT 1 slowed down the arms race and led to further negotiations (SALT 2, in 1979). It ensured that neither side had a decisive advantage. However, Détente had limits. The superpowers still targeted nuclear weapons at each other and competed for influence in the world.

Now try this

Why were the USA and the USSR now willing to talk? Give **two** reasons for each country.

Exam overview

This page introduces you to the main features and requirements of the Paper 1 Section B exam paper for Conflict and tension between East and West, 1945–1972.

About Paper 1

- Paper 1 is for your period study and your wider world depth study.

- Section B of the paper will be on your wider world depth study, which is Conflict and tension between East and West, 1945–1972.

- Section B will include questions about other wider world depth study options. You should **only** answer the questions about Conflict and tension between East and West, 1945–1972.

- You will receive two documents: a question paper which will contain the questions and sources, and an answer booklet.

The Paper 1 exam lasts for 1 hour 45 minutes (105 minutes). There are 84 marks in total: 40 marks for Section A; **40 marks for Section B, plus 4 marks for spelling, punctuation and grammar.** You should spend about 50 minutes on Section A and **50 minutes on Section B**, with 5 minutes to check your answers.

Here we are focusing on Section B and your wider world depth study. However, the same exam paper will also include Section A, where you will answer questions on your period study.

The questions

The questions for Paper 1 Section B will always follow this pattern:

You can see examples of all four questions on pages 32–37, and in the practice questions on pages 38–47.

Question 15
Study **Source G**.
Source G… How do you know?
Explain your answer using **Source G**
and your contextual knowledge.   **(4 marks)**

Question 15 targets AO3. AO3 is about analysing, evaluating and using sources to make substantiated judgements. Spend about 6 minutes on this question, which focuses on **analysing a source** and using your own **contextual knowledge.**

Question 16
Study **Sources H** and **J**.
How useful are **Sources H** and **J** to a historian studying… ?
Explain your answer using **Sources H** and **J** and your contextual knowledge.   **(12 marks)**

Question 16 also targets AO3. Spend about 14 minutes on this question, which is about **evaluating sources** and using your own **contextual knowledge.**

Question 17
Write an account...   **(8 marks)**

Question 17 targets AO1 and AO2. AO1 is about showing your knowledge and understanding of the key features and characteristics of the topic. AO2 is about explaining and analysing historical events using second order concepts such as causation, consequence, change, continuity, similarity and difference. Spend about 10 minutes on this question, which requires you to write a **narrative account**.

Question 18
[Statement]
How far do you agree with this statement?
Explain your answer.
          (16 marks, plus 4 marks for SPaG)

Question 18 also targets AO1 and AO2. Spend about 20 minutes on this question, which requires you to make a **judgement** in an **extended response**. Up to 4 marks are available for **spelling, punctuation and grammar** (SPaG).

Source skills

Questions 15 and 16 are based on **sources**. Question 15 asks you to **analyse one source**, and Question 16 asks you to **evaluate the usefulness of two different sources**.

What is a source?

A source is something that comes from the time period or event it describes.

A source can be text, such as:

- an account written by someone at the time, such as a letter or diary
- a speech
- a book or government report
- a poem or work of fiction
- a newspaper or magazine article.

It might also be visual, such as:

- a cartoon, photograph, poster or painting
- a plan of a building
- an advertisement
- an object such as a coin or postcard.

Contextual knowledge

✓ Questions 15 and 16 will both ask you to explain your answer using the sources and your **contextual knowledge**.

✓ This means that you need to think about what you know about the event or development and how the sources fit with what you know.

✓ Only use knowledge that is **relevant** to the topic in the question and that is linked to what is contained in the source itself.

Analysing sources

Analysing the source means working out what it's saying. For example, Question 15 asks you to look at a source and use your contextual knowledge to explain how it conveys a particular idea. To do this, think about:

- What is the **intended message** (purpose) of the source?
- What else can we **infer** (work out) from it? Remember, this may not be something the person who created the source intended!
- What can we tell from the **provenance** (origin and nature) of the source?
- Does the information in the source agree with your **contextual knowledge**? What does this tell you?

Evaluating sources

To evaluate the **usefulness** of a source, you need to look at the content, provenance and context as well as the source itself. For example, Question 16 asks you to evaluate the usefulness of two sources.

 Content
- What information in the sources is relevant to the enquiry?

            Underline and annotate information in the source to help you with this.

- How useful is this information?

 Provenance
- Nature: the type of source it is.
- Origins: who produced it and when.
- Purpose: the reason the source was created.

            Remember that this isn't necessarily about the amount of information given. A small piece of information can be very useful!

- How do these things impact on the usefulness of the source?

            Remember that an unreliable source can still be useful.

 Context
- Use your own knowledge of the enquiry topic to evaluate the source.
- Is the information in the source accurate compared with what you know?

            Remember to think about what information is missing from the source as well as what's included.

29

Source G

This source is referred to in the worked example on page 32.

SECTION B

Conflict and tension between East and West, 1945–1972

Source G A cartoon from the *Daily Mail* newspaper about the Berlin Blockade, April 1949. The aeroplanes are labelled 'Increased Air Lift', whilst out of Berlin come 'Scares', 'Lies' and 'Rumours'.

You will be given short details on where the source comes from. In this case, the type of source and where and when it was produced.

You will be given some information about the source. In this case, you are told that the source is about the Berlin Blockade.

Sources H and J

These sources are referred to in the worked examples on pages 33 and 34.

Source H   A British newspaper cartoon from 30 October 1945 showing (left–right) US President Truman, British prime minister Clement Attlee and Russian leader Josef Stalin. Truman presents his '12 points' for international peace.

"WHY CAN'T WE WORK TOGETHER IN MUTUAL TRUST & CONFIDENCE?"

Annotate the sources with your ideas. If the source is an image, like this one, think about the details you can see and what they might mean.

Source J   From the 'Novikov Telegram', 27 September 1946. The Soviet ambassador in Washington was asked to report to Moscow on US attitudes to the USSR.

> US policy has been characterised in the postwar period by a desire for world domination. All these steps to preserve the great military potential are not an end in itself, of course. They are intended only to prepare conditions to win world domination in a new war being planned by the warlike circles of American imperialism…

If the source is a text extract, underline or highlight any important words or phrases and annotate them.

Question 15: analysing sources

Question 15 on your exam paper will ask you to explain 'How you know ....' something about a source, using the source and your own knowledge of the **historical context**. There are 4 marks available for this question.

🔗 **Links** You can revise the Berlin Blockade on page 9.

Worked example

Study **Source G** on page 30.

Source G is critical of the Berlin Blockade. How do you know?

Explain your answer using **Source G** and your contextual knowledge. **(4 marks)**

Analysing a source

Analysing a source means working out what it means, including meanings that aren't directly shown.

✓ Think about what is suggested or implied by the source.

✓ Look at the **context** and **provenance** of the source too.

You need to **explain** how the source supports the statement in the question by:

✓ referring to details in the source and linking them to your contextual knowledge.

For more on analysing sources, turn to page 29.

Sample answer

I know the cartoon is critical of the Berlin Blockade. This is because it shows aeroplanes flying in and scares and rumours flying out. It also shows guards standing by a barrier that says to 'Keep Out'.

The student describes the picture and highlights some relevant information, but they only give limited analysis of the message of the cartoon.

The student needs to use contextual knowledge to explain what the details in the source are referring to.

Improved answer

I know the cartoon is critical of the Berlin Blockade because of the different images used to show the USA's and USSR's reactions to it. An endless line of aeroplanes can be seen flying into Berlin from the left (the West), which are labelled 'increased airlift'. In contrast, bats are seen flying out of the city from the right (the East) and are labelled 'scares', 'lies' and 'rumours'. This ridicules Stalin's attempts to force the West to back down and shows how little positive action was coming from the East.

The Blockade was a reaction to the West uniting their parts of Berlin and introducing a single new currency, helping West Germans to rebuild their lives. The Berlin Airlift showed the Allies as peaceful and generous. They would not back down to Soviet bullying. It was an important propaganda victory. Published in a British newspaper almost a year into the blockade, the cartoon is clearly supporting the West.

Think about what you can see and then move on to think about what it **suggests**. Don't just describe the source – you need to go further and show you understand what the author or artist is trying to say.

This answer includes relevant and detailed knowledge of the **historical context** of the source, in this case the reasons for, and the international response to, the Berlin Blockade.

Consider the intended **audience**, **message** and **the reason** the source was produced (its purpose). Also think about **when** it was produced as this context is vital for analysing the source, not just describing it.

Question 16: evaluating usefulness 1

Question 16 on your exam paper will ask you to evaluate the usefulness of two sources. There are 12 marks available for this question.

Worked example

Study **Sources H** and **J** on page 31.

How useful are **Sources H** and **J** to a historian studying the impact of the dropping of the atom bomb on international relations?

Explain your answer using **Sources H** and **J** and your contextual knowledge.

(12 marks)

 Turn to page 4 to revise the dropping of the atom bomb.

Evaluating the usefulness of sources

To judge the usefulness of a source, you need to think about the content of the source, and its provenance.

To evaluate the **content**, look carefully at the source and what it shows. How would it help someone understand the topic mentioned in the question? What details are included? Compare these details with your historical knowledge. Is there anything you would expect to see that isn't there?

To judge the **provenance**, think about what the source is, where it came from, and what it was intended for (its purpose).

You have two sources to consider, so evaluate the pros and cons of each. Do the sources complement each other? (This means does using both together gives you a fuller picture?)

For more on evaluating sources, turn to page 29.

Compare this answer with an improved version on the next page.

Sample answer

Sources H and J are both useful for a historian studying the impact of the dropping of the atom bomb on international relations.

Source H shows Truman presenting his '12 points' plan for peace to Stalin and Attlee. He is holding an atom bomb labelled 'PRIVATE' as he is keeping the bomb secret. Truman is asking 'Why can't we work together in mutual trust and confidence?' The source is useful because it shows what British people thought about this secrecy soon after it happened.

Source J is useful as it tells us Soviet views at the time. Novikov's telegram says the USA had a 'desire for world domination'. This telegram went to the Soviet leaders and gives a clear idea of their feelings towards the West. The USA were preparing for 'a new war' of 'American imperialism'. It accuses the Americans of being 'warlike'.

Be careful not to just describe what you can see in the source. This part of the answer identifies some good details, but the student needs to analyse what these details tell us and think about **how useful** the source is to a historian studying the impact of the dropping of the atom bomb.

The student begins to **evaluate** the usefulness of the sources, but this part of the answer needs to be developed further.

The student begins to **evaluate** the source by thinking about the author and what he was trying to do when he wrote this telegram. However, the student does not fully explain the question of usefulness by discussing what it tells us about the impact of the dropping of the atom bomb.

Question 16: evaluating usefulness 2

This page has an improved version of the answer given on page 33.

Improved answer

Both Sources H and J are useful for a historian studying the impact of the dropping of the atom bomb on international relations. They both present critical views of US diplomacy, suggesting that the bomb was partly responsible for the tensions that existed in 1945.

Source H is a British cartoon produced in October 1945, following the Potsdam Conference and US President Truman's '12 Points'. It is useful because it shows that US allies – not just the Soviets – were critical of US policy. It depicts a smiling Truman presenting his '12 points' plan for peace to Stalin and Attlee. At the same time, he is holding an atom bomb labelled 'PRIVATE'. Truman delayed the Potsdam talks until the USA had successfully tested its new weapon to put the USA in a stronger position. Truman is asking 'Why can't we work together in mutual trust and confidence?' while keeping secrets from his fellow leaders.

Source H is useful because it suggests what popular opinion in Britain may have been about this secrecy, but it is limited in its use because it could be just the cartoonist's view. The source does not tell us about either US or Soviet opinions and motives. Newspapers rely on sensation to sell so the cartoonist may have been deliberately controversial. For example, Churchill's 'Iron Curtain' speech of 1946 suggests an entirely different view of US and Soviet policy.

Source J is useful as it gives us an insight into Soviet views at the time. It also supports Source H's suspicion of US motives and actions. Novikov was based in the USA and his telegram suggests that US policy was driven by a 'desire for world domination'. This is supported by Truman's determination to keep his new weapon firmly in the hands of the USA. This telegram went straight to the Soviet government in Moscow, and presents a clear idea of Soviet attitudes towards the West. However, it is also therefore less likely to be unbiased. It does not give a true indication of US motives and actions. A report from the US ambassador in Moscow, sent a few months before, shows that US fear of Soviet intentions was also very real.

Start with a clear **introductory statement** that links directly to the question. The student then goes on to look at the **provenance** of the first source and consider what that tells us.

Contextual knowledge

Don't forget that this question also requires you to include your contextual knowledge. You need to show that you understand what was going on at the time the sources were created and how this might impact on their usefulness. For example, did the creator of the source have all the information, or were they biased? Your contextual knowledge must be directly relevant to this question.

Relate the details in the source to your own **contextual knowledge**. Here the student links the depiction of Truman in the cartoon with the events of the Potsdam Conference.

Make sure that you evaluate the source by considering its **content** and **purpose**. Here the student explains the impact of the cartoonist's and newspaper's purpose on usefulness and considers how typical the opinions presented in the cartoon might have been.

Focus on evaluating and making judgements about the **usefulness** of the sources, not just describing them. Make sure you keep relating the source to your contextual knowledge.

This answer uses specific language, such as: insight, depict, presents. Using specific language can make your argument clearer and your answer more focused.

Question 17: narrative account

Question 17 on your exam paper requires you to write a narrative account analysing how and why a historical event happened. There are 8 marks available for this question.

Worked example

Write an account of how the Cuban Revolution became an international crisis in 1959.

(8 marks)

 Links You can revise the Cuban Revolution and missile crisis that followed on pages 21–23.

What is a narrative account?

A **narrative account** is not simply a description of what happened. To write a successful narrative account you need to:

 think about **key elements** of the event and how they were **connected**

 consider what you have been asked to do – you may need to think about **cause, change, continuity** and/or **consequence** here

 use your **own knowledge** of the period

structure your narrative logically, so it clearly explains the **sequence** of events.

Sample answer

Castro's revolution in Cuba in 1959 directly threatened the USA. When the USSR began supporting Castro, it rapidly became part of the Cold War and almost led to nuclear war. This was known as MAD – Mutually Assured Destruction.

Fidel Castro replaced the Cuban government that was backed by the USA with a socialist one in 1959. His government seized US-owned businesses for the state, angering the USA. Tension increased further when Castro secured trade deals with the USA's Cold War rival, the USSR.

As a result of this, the USA banned all trade with Cuba in an attempt to force Castro to back down. The USA was concerned that a government with communist support now existed just 100 miles from US land. In January 1961, the USA broke off diplomatic relations as well.

This was followed by a failed US-backed invasion of Cuba in April 1961, known as the 'Bay of Pigs' incident. This pushed Castro further towards his Soviet ally. Castro declared himself communist and asked the Soviets to help defend Cuba from the USA. In September, Khrushchev announced in response that the Soviets would provide arms to Cuba.

In reaction, Kennedy warned Khrushchev not to use Cuba as a base to threaten the USA from. However, in October 1962 the USA discovered launch pads on Cuba for missiles that could strike their cities. If the Soviets put nuclear missiles on Cuba, the US mainland would be directly under threat for the first time. When Soviet ships sailed towards Cuba, the Cuban Missile Crisis began – and no one knew what might happen as a result.

In conclusion, the Cuban Revolution led to tensions with the USA. These were increased when Castro allied with the USSR, turning a local revolution into an international crisis when the USSR tried to place nuclear missiles on Cuba.

Start with a **clear introduction** which relates to the question and signposts your argument. A sentence or two is enough for this.

Use your **own knowledge** of the period. Here, the information about Castro's actions shows the use of relevant knowledge.

 Links You can revise Castro's revolution on page 21.

This is a clear account of **how one thing led to another**, linking the event – in this case Castro's actions – to the result, in this case, the impact on relations with the USA.

Explain clearly how the events led to the consequence. Here, the student not only explains in sequence what happened but explains why these events were important, and how the events led to an international crisis.

Your answer should relate to the question being asked. This is a clear and detailed explanation of the effect of the Cuban Revolution on international relations.

Question 18: extended response 1

Question 18 on your exam paper will ask you to write an **extended response** showing a sustained line of reasoning and making a judgement. You will be given a statement and asked **how far** you agree with it. There are 16 marks available for this question, plus four marks for spelling, punctuation, grammar and use of historical terminology.

Worked example

'The main reason for the tension between East and West in Europe in the 1950s was the actions of the USA and its allies.'
How far do you agree with this statement?
Explain your answer.

(16 marks plus 4 marks for SPaG)

🔗 **Links**   You can revise this period on pages 13–18.

It can be helpful to write a list of points **for** and **against** the judgement in the question before you start writing your answer.

'How far...' questions

This question asks you to weigh **evidence** to come up with an argument – a **line of reasoning**. You need to:

- ✓ describe any evidence that supports the statement in the question, explaining why it **supports** the statement
- ✓ do the same for any evidence that **contradicts** the statement
- ✓ develop a **sustained** line of reasoning – 'sustained' means you need to present a clear, logical argument **throughout your answer**
- ✓ make a **judgement** – you need to decide 'how far' you agree by reaching a conclusion based on the evidence and reasoning in your answer.

Sample answer

I believe that the USSR was more to blame than the USA for tensions between East and West in Europe in the 1950s.

The West cannot be blamed for the increased tensions with the East in this period. The USSR continued to try to beat the USA in the arms race. By 1961 the USSR had created the largest bomb ever seen. The explosion was the same size as all the explosives used in the Second World War put together. Khrushchev ordered the West to leave Berlin in 1958, putting tensions at their highest.

When Stalin died in 1953, Khrushchev called for 'peaceful co-existence'. This encouraged Eastern bloc countries such as Poland to introduce their own reforms. Instead of easing tensions, the actions of the USSR increased them. The Warsaw Pact, which was formed in 1955, divided Europe into two sides. When Hungary withdrew from the Pact in 1956, the Hungarian uprising was brutally crushed by the USSR. The USA and its allies did not respond, which showed how determined they were not to increase tensions further.

In conclusion, the actions of the USSR were more important than the actions of the USA and its allies in explaining the tensions between East and West.

Compare this answer with an improved version on the next page.

Start your answer with a **clear statement**, signposting your argument.

Remember that you should only include information that is **relevant** to the question. This answer contains facts that are not directly relevant to evaluating the judgement in the question. Rather than describing the arms race the answer should examine **what impact** it had on tensions between East and West.

All your points should be supported with **evidence**. Here, the student gives basic evidence but this could be expanded.

Make sure that you **examine both sides** of the argument. Here, the student develops a line of argument but it is limited to the actions of the USSR, and only briefly discusses any actions of the USA and its allies, as mentioned in the question.

Question 18: extended response 2

This page has an improved version of the answer on page 36.

Improved answer

Although the actions of the USA and its allies may have pushed the USSR into its own actions, I believe that the USSR was more to blame for tensions between East and West in Europe in the 1950s than the USA.

The formation of NATO in 1949 caused tensions between East and West in the 1950s, as the USA agreed to work with Western European powers to limit the expansion of communism. The USSR saw this as a threat to their own interests. When West Germany joined NATO in 1955, this was too much for the USSR. The USSR set up the Warsaw Pact, dividing Europe into two sides facing each other over the 'Iron Curtain'. Also, in order to keep ahead in the arms race, in 1952 the USA tested the first hydrogen bomb. This caused both sides to push for more powerful weapons and led to the possibility of 'mutually assured destruction'. The USSR caught up in 1953 and by 1961 had created the largest bomb ever seen. Nuclear war was a real fear for the people of East and West.

However, Western actions cannot be blamed for the increased tensions caused by the actions of the USSR in this period. Stalin's death in 1953 led to a period of de-Stalinisation within the USSR as Khrushchev called for 'peaceful co-existence' and a relaxation of persecution. This encouraged Eastern bloc countries such as Poland to introduce their own reforms. This could have helped to ease tensions but, when Hungary withdrew from the Warsaw Pact in 1956, Khrushchev reacted brutally. The Hungarian uprising was crushed by the USSR. The lack of response from the USA and its allies shows how determined they were not to increase tensions further. Finally, in 1958, tensions reached crisis point when Khrushchev issued the Berlin Ultimatum in order to try to force the West out of Berlin.

In conclusion, I would argue that the actions of the USA and its allies were an important factor. However, the reaction and further actions of the USSR were more important in explaining the tensions between East and West – dividing Europe into two sides and brutally crushing any resistance.

This introduction clearly signposts that the answer will consider **both sides** of the argument.

Highlighting key points raised by the statement will help you focus on the arguments that you need to **evaluate** to make your judgement.

This paragraph explores the actions of the USA and its allies in the early 1950s and how this increased tensions between East and West.

Starting a paragraph with words and phrases such as 'However' or 'On the other hand' clearly demonstrates that you are moving on to another part of your argument, and shows that your answer is following a clear **structure** and has a **sustained line of reasoning**.

Remember that for this question four additional marks are available for good **spelling, grammar, punctuation** and use of historical **terminology**.

Use specific **historical vocabulary**, such as: NATO, Warsaw Pact, arms race, de-Stalinisation, 'peaceful co-existence' to make sure your answer is really focused.

Finish with a clear **conclusion**, summarising the main arguments and stating clearly 'how far' you agree with the statement.

Practice

You will need to refer to the source below in your answer to question 15 on page 40.

SECTION B

Conflict and tension between East and West, 1945–1972

Source G A poster about the communist-backed invasion of South Korea, published in the early 1950s by the US Information Agency.

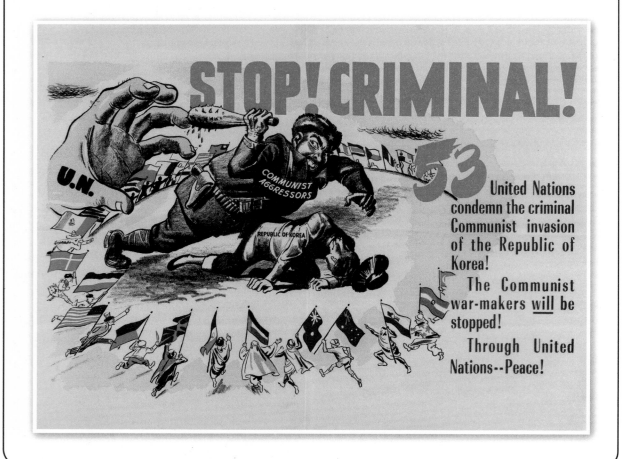

Practice

You will need to refer to the sources below in your answer to question 16 on page 41.

Source H   A British cartoon published in a national newspaper on 6 March 1946, the day after Churchill's 'Iron Curtain' speech. It shows Winston Churchill looking under the 'Iron Curtain' while armed guards peer over the wall. 'Joe' refers to Joseph Stalin, leader of the USSR.

Source J   From the 'Iron Curtain' speech by former British prime minister Winston Churchill, given to an American audience on a visit to the USA on 5 March 1946.

An iron curtain has descended across the Continent. Behind that line lie all the capitals of the ancient states of Central and East Europe. The populations around them lie in what I must call the Soviet sphere, and all are subject in one form or another, not only to Soviet influence but to a high measure of control from Moscow. I do not believe that Soviet Russia desires war. What they desire is the fruits of war and the indefinite expansion of their powers and doctrines.

Practice

Put your skills and knowledge into practice with the following question. You will need to refer to Source G on page 38 in your answer.

> **15** Study **Source G**.
>
> **Source G** supports US involvement in Korea. How do you know?
>
> Explain your answer using **Source G** and your contextual knowledge. **(4 marks)**
>
> **Guided** I know the poster supports US involvement in Korea because it shows a giant 'communist aggressor' attacking the 'Republic of Korea', which is lying on the ground. The message is
>
> ....
>
> ....
>
> ....
>
> ....
>
> ....
>
> ....
>
> ....
>
> ....
>
> ....
>
> ....
>
> ....
>
> ....
>
> ....
>
> ....
>
> ....
>
> ....

You have 1 hour 45 minutes for the **whole** of Paper 1, which means you have 50 minutes for Section B. You should use the time carefully to answer all the questions fully. In the exam, remember to leave 5 minutes to check your work when you've finished both Sections A and B.

Spend about 6 minutes on this answer. You need to identify features in the source and use your own knowledge.

 Links You can revise the Korean War on page 11.

You can revise how to analyse sources on page 29.

Remember to make **inferences** from the source to show you are analysing it. This means working out something that isn't shown directly. An example of a suitable inference might be that 'The USA was keen not to be seen as acting alone. With UN support, they could say the international community was with them.'

Make a claim based on evidence you take from the source (in this case the poster) on the intended **purpose** of the source: who its message was aimed at and why.

Link your argument to your **contextual knowledge** of the period.

Make sure you give **examples** of details from the source to back up what you say.

Practice

Put your skills and knowledge into practice with the following question. You will need to refer to Sources H and J on page 39 in your answer.

16 Study **Sources H** and **J**.

How useful are **Sources H** and **J** to a historian studying the tensions in post-war Europe?

Explain your answer, using **Sources H** and **J** and your contextual knowledge. **(12 marks)**

Guided   Both Sources H and J are useful for finding out

about the tensions in post-war Europe.

....

....

....

....

....

....

....

....

....

....

....

....

....

....

....

....

....

....

....

....

You should spend about 14 minutes on this answer.

'Useful' means you have to judge what the source tells you about the question you are being asked. You will also need to think about what the problems with the source could be.

 Links You can revise post-war tensions on pages 4–6.

You can revise how to evaluate sources on page 29.

Remember, you need to identify and **evaluate** the pros and cons of **both** sources and make a judgement. You can consider the sources separately in your answer, or use them together to explain a point.

Make sure you include some examples from your **contextual knowledge**. Don't just rely on the content and provenance of the sources.

Practice

Use this page to continue your answer to question 16.

....

....

....

....

....

....

....

Think: Are there any aspects of the sources that make them less **useful**? You might find it helpful to consider the **provenance** of the two sources here.

....

....

....

....

....

....

....

....

....

....

....

....

....

....

....

....

....

....

....

....

....

Practice

Put your skills and knowledge into practice with the following question.

17 Write an account of how events in Czechoslovakia became an international crisis in 1968.

(8 marks)

Guided   Life behind the 'Iron Curtain' was tightly controlled and harsh. Soviet control in Czechoslovakia

....

....

....

....

....

....

....

....

....

....

....

....

....

....

....

....

....

....

....

....

....

....

....

You should spend about 10 minutes on this question.

'Write an account' means you have to give a narrative that **explains the connections**, and does not just describe what happened.

Links You can revise the Prague Spring on page 24.

Keep your answer focused on the question. You might remember lots of detail about the Prague Spring, but you need to focus on why it developed into an international crisis.

Make sure you use your **own knowledge** of the period, by describing how factors combined to bring about an outcome – in this case how different factors came together and resulted in the Soviet invasion of Czechoslovakia.

Make sure your answer **analyses the links** between factors. Try to use phrases such as: 'this was because', 'this led to', 'the result of this was ...', 'the factors that caused this were ...'. This will help you make sure that your answer follows a **logical structure**.

Practice

Use this page to continue your answer to question 17.

....

....

....

....

....

....

....

....

....

....

....

....

....

Question 17 has a focus on **how tension and conflict increased** from the first event to the international crisis at the end. It is a good idea to identify points at which tension increased and explain them.

You may be able to identify some events that were more important than others in leading to or causing the international crisis. This will make your analysis stronger.

10 minutes is not very long so remember to **keep your account focused**. Resist the temptation to write everything you can remember about the topic.

Practice

Put your skills and knowledge into practice with the following question.

18 'The main reason for Détente by 1972 was the Cuban Missile Crisis.'

How far do you agree with this statement?

Explain your answer.

(16 marks, plus 4 marks for SPaG)

Guided There were a number of causes that came

together to lead to Détente by 1972. The Cuban Missile

Crisis – and the threat of nuclear war – was perhaps the

biggest, but it was not the only cause.

....

....

....

....

....

....

....

....

....

....

....

....

....

....

....

....

....

....

....

....

You should spend about 20 minutes on this question.

Remember, this question is where you will also receive marks for your **spelling, punctuation and grammar**. So, write and check your work carefully!

Make sure your answer stays focused on the question you have been asked and keep your answer relevant in a **sustained** way. Don't just write everything you know about the topic.

Links You can revise the reasons for Détente on page 27.

This is a 'how far' question so you need to come up with a **balanced** response: ideas and evidence that support the statement, as well as points that do not.

Plan your answer before you start writing. List factors that support the statement in the question and list other factors that go against the statement.

Practice

Use this page to continue your answer to question 18.

....

....

....

....

....

....

....

....

....

....

....

....

....

....

....

....

....

....

....

....

....

....

....

It is a good idea to signpost your answer by beginning each paragraph with a clear statement to give the reader an idea of how the answer will develop. For example, 'The cost of the Cold War was an important factor because...' and 'However, there were other factors that led to Détente, such as...'

This will make it easier to write and will make your answer easier to understand. It will also show that you are developing **a clear line of reasoning** and show that you are considering **evidence** from both sides.

Practice

Use this page to continue your answer to question 18.

....
....
....
....
....
....
....
....
....
....
....
....
....
....
....
....
....
....
....
....
....
....
....
....
....
....

End your answer with a conclusion, giving a clear **judgement** about **how far** you agree with the statement in the question.

ANSWERS

Where an exemplar answer is given, this is not necessarily the only correct response. In most cases there is a range of responses that can gain full marks.

SUBJECT CONTENT

The origins of the Cold War

1. Aims of the key leaders

For example:
- Churchill: Wanted a free and democratic Poland. This threatened Stalin's desire to expand westward and spread communism in Europe.
- Roosevelt: Wanted democracy in Europe and capitalist nations to trade with. This was against Stalin's wish to put communist 'democracies' in Eastern Europe.
- Stalin: Wanted to make sure Germany would never invade the USSR again. This was against the other leaders' desire to rebuild Germany.

2. Attitudes and ideologies

Any three from:
- The USA had supported the government against the communists in the Russian Civil War.
- The USA feared the spread of communist ideas and revolution.
- The USA supported free elections, the Soviets did not.
- The USA supported individual freedoms and self-government, the Soviets did not.
- The Soviet communists saw capitalism as selfish and unfair.
- The USA faced panic at home in the 'Red Scare'.

3. Yalta and Potsdam conferences

Yalta: The Allies wanted a weak post-war Germany. So, at Yalta, they agreed to reduce it in size, to divide it up and to take reparations to pay for the war. Germany would also be demilitarised: its armed forces would be limited. A United Nations would be set up to settle future arguments. Stalin agreed to declare war on Japan. However, the Allies had to compromise over Poland: it would remain under Soviet influence, but Stalin agreed it would be 'democratic'.

Potsdam: Once Germany had surrendered, the Allies built on the Yalta agreements at Potsdam. A council was set up to help rebuild Europe. The Nazi Party was officially banned, and surviving war criminals were to be prosecuted. Germany and Berlin were both split into four zones, with each zone run by one of the Allies. Each country was to take reparations from their own zones, though the Soviets also got a quarter of the output of the other zones.

4. Dropping the bomb

For example, any three from:
- Truman kept the bomb a secret and delayed the Potsdam Conference until the bomb was ready. This increased suspicion and fear within the USSR of Truman's motives.
- It encouraged Truman to be more determined to get his way in the talks, which in turn made Stalin more determined to protect the USSR with a buffer zone.
- It made Stalin determined to catch up with US technology and build a Soviet bomb, leading to rivalry.
- Both powers became even more suspicious of each other, and believed they were going to be attacked. This is seen in the Kennan and Novikov reports.

5. The division of Germany

Any three from:
- Poland's borders giving more land to the USSR.
- Reparations: how far to 'punish' and cripple Germany, and how much the USSR got.
- The division of Germany into different zones, with a single united economy.
- The wish for Poland to have free, democratic elections.

6. Soviet expansion

After the Second World War ended, Stalin's Red Army occupied much of Eastern Europe. Stalin gained control of Eastern Europe by setting up one-party communist states in Poland, Czechoslovakia, Hungary, Romania and Bulgaria using 'salami tactics'. The communists fixed the elections and shut down opposing parties, using force and spreading fear. Stalin arrested thousands of Polish non-communists. In Hungary, the secret police imprisoned and executed their opponents. Albania and Yugoslavia also deposed their rulers to become communist, and looked to Stalin for support, though they remained independent of Soviet control.

7. US policies

The USA hoped that aid from the Marshall Plan would allow Western Europe to recover from the war. This would improve living standards and reduce support for Europe's communist parties, who appealed to those people with no money or jobs.

8. Stalin's reaction

Stalin was determined to protect the USSR against threats from the West, especially the USA. He formed Cominform in 1947 and Comecon in 1949 to counter the Truman Doctrine and the Marshall Plan. He wanted this communist 'Eastern bloc' to act as a buffer zone, keeping the USSR safe from attack. When Tito approached the USA for Marshall Plan aid for Yugoslavia, it made the communists look weak and meant that other communist states might also look to the USA for support. It was a direct challenge to Stalin's control and threatened to increase US influence in Eastern Europe. Stalin was furious and expelled Yugoslavia from Cominform.

9. The Berlin Blockade

For example, any three from:
- Stalin wanted to prove that the USSR could stop a divided Germany working.
- Stalin was angry that Bizonia had been created without his knowledge.
- West Germany was richer than East Germany. Stalin wanted Germany to be weak.
- West Berlin was dependent on East Germany for supplies.

The development of the Cold War

10. Revolution in China

China was a huge, powerful country and its 'fall' to communism was a significant factor in boosting Eastern communism against the West. The USSR took advantage through the Treaty of Friendship to boost its own economy. The USA had supported China's official government against the communists, and refused to acknowledge the new PRC. This increased tensions between East and West. The CCP's victory shocked the West and led to preparations for war. It was seen as a failure for Truman's policy of containment. The West was worried that such a powerful country had become communist, and was concerned communism might spread further in Asia. So the West invested in Taiwan and Japan to make sure this did not happen. This reaction increased tensions further.

11. The Korean War, 1950–53

1 Your flowchart should cover the following points:
- At Potsdam (1945), Korea was divided in two: the communist North, supported by the USSR, and the capitalist South, allied to the USA.
- Both Kim in the North and Rhee in the South wanted to reunite Korea under their own leadership. Kim had strong links to the USSR and was keen to spread communism to the South.
- Kim asked the Soviets to back an invasion (1949). Stalin encouraged China, a new and powerful communist country, to get involved.

- When the North invaded in 1950, the USA stood firm in support of South Korea and against the spread of communism. It used its influence in the UN to condemn Kim's actions.
- A US-led UN force was sent to boost South Korea and to oppose the North. Success encouraged the USA to move from containment of communism to invading the North.
- When UN forces entered North Korea, Chinese forces counterattacked and drove them back to the 38th parallel. The fighting turned into a stalemate.

2 The key outcome of the Korean War was that it became clear that the USA and the USSR wanted to avoid a direct war with each other, especially because a war might involve nuclear weapons.

12. The Vietnam War, 1955–75

1 Your flowchart should cover the following points:
- At Geneva (1954), the USA refused to sign the agreement to accept a communist North Vietnam.
- The communist Vietcong in South Vietnam built up forces to overthrow the US-backed ruler, Diem. They were backed by Chinese and Soviet support.
- The USA retaliated by increasing support for South Vietnam and removing the corrupt Diem in 1963.
- After Kennedy's assassination in 1963, Johnson declared full military involvement in Vietnam.
- The war dragged on as US forces were unable to fight effectively against the Vietcong in the dense jungle terrain.

2 The USA was worried about the spread of communism if Vietnam became communist. This 'domino' effect made the USA more determined than ever to contain the threat, and this led to full-scale war in Vietnam. As China and the USSR sent more and more support to North Vietnam, this increased tensions between East and West.

13. The arms race

For example, any three from:
- Brinkmanship: leaders pushed events close to the edge of conflict, hoping that their rival would not use nuclear weapons, which would be catastrophic.
- MAD: the two superpowers became less willing to risk all-out war and Mutually Assured Destruction.
- Defence costs on both sides continued to rise as each side feared letting the other get ahead of them in the arms race. Weapons became bigger and bigger.
- The fear of nuclear attack increased tensions and fears. Governments ran campaigns to prepare their citizens for a nuclear attack.

14. The space race

For example, any two from:
- The space race provided a non-military battleground to compete on. Both sides raced to prove the dominance of their way of life through scientific achievement.
- Both sides wanted to be seen as the 'leader' of the world and the space race formed part of this leadership. Russian successes drove the USA to try to outdo their rival.
- It was also an important part of the escalating arms race. The rocket technology led to more powerful and longer-ranged delivery methods for their nuclear weapons. This would have further strengthened tensions and increased military rivalry.
- The Polaris missile developed by the USA meant that the USSR could not be sure where US missiles might launch from, as they could be launched by submarine, increasing fears.

15. NATO and the Warsaw Pact

The formation of NATO provoked the Soviets into forming the Warsaw Pact, and this led to the division of Europe into two armed alliances.

16. Hungary: protest and reform

Many Hungarians were prepared to protest because they did not like communist rule. Hungary's dictator Mátyás Rákosi, who was known as the 'Bald Butcher', was unpopular. Rákosi's harsh policies meant that up to 5% of the population was imprisoned. Another reason was that food and industrial products were being taken to the USSR.

By protesting, Hungarians hoped to end these policies and improve their lives. In addition, Khrushchev's secret speech persuaded many Hungarians that it was possible to protest against the regime without fear of arrest. Finally, the withdrawal of Soviet troops from Austria in 1955 may have persuaded some Hungarians that protest could result in a Soviet retreat from Hungary as well.

17. Soviet reaction

a) Hungary leaving would encourage others and the Eastern bloc would collapse. It threatened communism.
b) The USA wouldn't risk nuclear war to defend a satellite state, so the USSR could act as it liked.

18. U2 Crisis and peace process

The U2 Crisis exposed the lack of trust between the superpowers. Khrushchev left the Paris Peace Summit. It effectively ended the 'Thaw'.

Transformation of the Cold War

19. Reasons for the Berlin Wall

Khrushchev built the Berlin Wall to end the refugee problem in Berlin. Thousands of East Germans were going to West Berlin and from there to West Germany. This created a skills shortage in East Germany. It was also humiliating for Khrushchev, because it seemed to demonstrate that ordinary people preferred capitalism to communism. Khrushchev could not enforce his ultimatum, as the USA prepared for nuclear war. The Wall also reduced the risk of war with the USA.

20. Kennedy's response

Kennedy is one of us. The USA will protect us against the USSR. Khrushchev beware! West Berlin = Freedom!

21. Castro's revolution

For Castro, any two from:
- Overthrew Batista and set up a socialist government
- Seized control of US businesses in Cuba
- Allied with the USSR
For the USA, any two from:
- Refused to talk to Castro
- Tried to assassinate Castro
- Banned all trade with Cuba
- The Bay of Pigs invasion

22. The Cuban Missile Crisis

Khrushchev: Khrushchev was to blame because he wanted to push Kennedy around and expand Soviet influence into the US backyard.
Kennedy: Kennedy was to blame because he had tried to invade Cuba and the USA would not talk with Castro, instead ordering the blockade.

23. Results of the crisis

The main outcome of the Cuban Missile Crisis was Détente. The crisis had come very close to nuclear war and both sides realised that this could not be allowed to happen again. A hotline was set up to allow the two leaders to talk. Treaties to limit nuclear weapons were signed during a period of decreasing hostility and tension.

24. Dubček and the Prague Spring

Any two from:
- The relaxation of controls on free speech and censorship encouraged a wave of criticism of communism that might spread.
- The increase in democracy threatened the power of the Communist Party and might lead to calls for reform elsewhere in the Warsaw Pact countries, such as Poland.
- If reforms to the economy succeeded, it would show that more capitalist economies worked better than more communist ones.
- A decrease in the power of the secret police weakened the Soviet grip on power.

25. The USSR's response

Any two from:
- The USA refused to support the Czechs, showing the USSR that it could act without challenge in the communist Eastern bloc.
- The invasion split the communist world in two, as countries horrified by Soviet imperialism allied themselves with China instead.
- The invasion discouraged countries in the Eastern bloc, like Poland, from reforming.
- Détente continued with barely an interruption, as the USA was more focused on Vietnam.

26. Sources of tension

a) The USA was determined to stop communism spreading and so fought its spread in Vietnam. As the war dragged on, mounting casualties increased tensions with the USSR.

b) Communism put the state first, not the people. This meant that their rights and freedoms were restricted, which the West did not like.

27. Détente and SALT 1

For the USA, any two from:
- Gained a stronger position to negotiate with both China and the USSR when relations between these countries broke down.
- Keen to avoid another Cuban crisis and prevent nuclear war: the hotline improved communication.
- Nixon promised to end US involvement in the Vietnam War: US power had not been enough to win the war against a weaker, but determined, rival.
- The arms race was expensive and the Partial Test Ban Treaty made a start on limiting weapons. The USA needed to focus on social issues at home and protests against foreign policy were frequent.

For the USSR, any two from:
- Felt vulnerable because of improved relations between China and the USA.
- Keen to avoid another Cuban crisis and prevent nuclear war: the hotline improved communication.
- Was looking for more indirect ways to influence events after Vietnam showed overwhelming force was not always enough to win wars.
- The arms race was expensive and the Partial Test Ban Treaty made a start on limiting weapons. The USSR faced bankruptcy if it continued spending as it was.

PRACTICE

40. Practice

15 I know the poster supports US involvement in Korea because it shows a giant 'communist aggressor' attacking the 'Republic of Korea', which is lying on the ground. The message is that this violent thug is bullying the small, weak Republic. The hand of the UN is clearly trying to hold the thug back. The figures are surrounded by smaller figures representing all the countries of the UN that voted in June 1950 to demand North Korea's withdrawal. This shows that the USA is not acting alone, and that the international community is united against communist aggression. The source is a poster so is designed to be seen by lots of people, in order to win public support for US involvement in Korea. It is propaganda aimed to justify the USA taking action against North Korea. It clearly calls the invaders 'Criminals' and strongly highlights the fact that '53' nations are united against the invasion. These nations are fighting to stop the North Korean 'war-makers' and for 'peace' in Korea.

41. Practice

16 Both Sources H and J are useful for studying tensions in post-war Europe. They give different views on the formation of the 'Iron Curtain', and together give a useful view of building tensions. Source H is a British cartoon from the day after Churchill's 'Iron Curtain' speech in 1946. It depicts the USSR full of construction and industry, hidden away behind an 'iron curtain' wall. On it is written 'No admittance by order Joe', as the Soviets try to hide their progress. On the other side of the wall is an empty Europe, apart from some ruins and a few people trying to see past the wall. Churchill is trying to peer under the wall. The suggestion is that he is jealous or suspicious of what is going on. This is different to Churchill's concerns in his speech, but does suggest the Soviets were being secretive.

Source J is an extract from Churchill's speech. He made this to an American audience during a visit to the USA. It gives a good insight into the West's suspicions of the USSR. The context of the speech also suggests that British and US interests were closely linked. Churchill is probably talking to people who share his concerns. Although he says he does not think that Stalin wants war, he does suggest that Stalin wants 'the fruits of war', to expand his power and to spread communist 'doctrines'. This is exactly what the West feared, with the 'Red Scares' in the USA and the formation of HUAC in 1938. The Red Army occupied a lot of Eastern Europe after the war and Stalin kept tight control to protect the USSR from future Western attacks. Satellite states were developing throughout Eastern Europe with communist one-party states, loyal to Moscow.

The sources give very useful insights into Western fears. Source H shows how communications and travel had been cut off by showing the wall cutting across a railway line and armed guards looking across. It suggests the secrecy of the Soviets. The humour, however, does suggest that perhaps some British people were less concerned with the Soviet threat. Churchill was known to be very anti-communist and was no longer prime minister at this time, so his views might not represent the view of the British people any more. Also, although Source H suggests that there may be more to the situation than Churchill admits, neither source really gives the Soviet viewpoint. The Novikov telegram gives a good idea of how the Soviets saw the West. Finally, we cannot be sure how common the cartoonist's view was. He may have had his own reasons for making Churchill look foolish.

43. Practice

17 Life behind the 'Iron Curtain' was tightly controlled and hard. Soviet control in Czechoslovakia had a bad effect on the country's economy and the people living there. The one-party government limited media through censorship and did not allow opposition. By the 1960s, communist rule was becoming increasingly unpopular, creating a crisis within Czechoslovakia.

This led to calls for reform from the people of Czechoslovakia. Czech economist Ota Šik's calls for reform attracted popular support. As a result, in January 1968, Alexander Dubček was placed in power. Dubček, a loyal communist, was a close friend of the Soviet leader Brezhnev and a supporter of the Warsaw Pact. However, he also believed in 'socialism with a human face'. He wanted to make communism work for his people.

The result of Dubček coming to power was the 'Prague Spring', which created a wider crisis for the USSR. Dubček introduced a number of reforms, relaxing controls and restrictions, and increasing democracy and freedom in Czechoslovakia. This led to increasing criticism of communism both within Czechoslovakia and within the Warsaw Pact countries, widening the problem to an international one for the USSR. Polish students called for similar reforms in Poland. Both Yugoslavia, and Romania which was another Warsaw Pact member, spoke out in support of Dubček. Brezhnev feared the reforms would destroy the Eastern bloc.

The crisis in Czechoslovakia became an international crisis. When Soviet pressure failed to stop Dubček's reforms, Brezhnev turned to force. On 20 August, Soviet forces invaded Czechoslovakia.

They claimed they were just restoring order. Dubček was arrested and replaced with a government more acceptable to Moscow. The USA condemned the invasion and cancelled a planned meeting between Brezhnev and the US president. The UN tried to pass a resolution to condemn the Soviet attack. In this way, the invasion triggered an international crisis.

45. Practice

Answers to Question 18 should:
- balance evidence to make a clear, logical argument
- give evidence that supports the statement and explain why
- give evidence that contradicts the statement and explain why
- make a judgement about which side of the argument is stronger – this is your 'how far'.

For example:

18 There were a number of causes that came together to lead to Détente by 1972. The Cuban Missile Crisis – and the threat of nuclear war – was perhaps the biggest, but it was not the only cause. Changing international relations, the experiences of conflict and cost were important too.

The Cuban Missile Crisis of 1962 brought the world to the edge of nuclear war but it also showed that neither superpower really wanted to use its nuclear weapons. Despite 'brinkmanship', both the USA and the USSR resisted launching missiles. They worked hard to make sure that another crisis would not happen. This led to early attempts to 'thaw' their relationship. A 'hotline' was set up to improve communication. There were attempts to limit the arms race, such as the Partial Test Ban Treaty in 1963. This was the start of Détente.

Another reason for Détente was the increasing tensions between the USSR and communist China. Khrushchev and Chairman Mao did not get on. The USA was keen to widen this split and build stronger ties with China. This encouraged the Soviets to build ties with the USA too, so they were not left alone. China's development of nuclear weapons in 1964 also changed the balance of power. This encouraged the USA and the USSR to cooperate: they no longer held the monopoly on nuclear weapons and hoped to limit their spread. In 1972, Nixon was the first US president to visit China.

The Korean and Vietnam wars showed the world that military strength and nuclear weapons were not enough to be sure of victory. This was another reason for Détente. Both superpowers looked for ways to secure their interests without risking direct conflict. The wars showed the value in improving relations. Finally, another key reason for Détente was the economic cost of the arms race. Along with the space race, which was increasing in intensity, the Cold War was a huge expense that neither superpower could afford by 1972. The cost had almost bankrupted the USSR and the USA faced social unrest and protests at home over inequality, poverty and its foreign policies. Billions of dollars were being wasted on weapons that would, they hoped, never be used. The cost of the arms race is perhaps the strongest factor as to why Détente was reached in the 1970s.

In conclusion, Détente had several causes, but the economic cost of the arms race was the greatest immediate one. However, Détente was made possible by the steps taken after the Cuban Missile Crisis, because of the scare of nuclear war. So, the Crisis was the greatest overall cause.

Notes

Notes

Published by Pearson Education Limited, 80 Strand, London, WC2R 0RL.

www.pearsonschoolsandfecolleges.co.uk

Text and illustrations © Pearson Education Ltd 2018
Produced by Just Content Ltd., Braintree, Essex
Typeset by PDQ Digital Media Solutions Ltd.
Cover illustration by Eoin Coveney

The right of Paul Martin to be identified as author of this work has been asserted by him in accordance with the Copyright, Designs and Patents Act 1988.

First published 2018

21 20 19 18
10 9 8 7 6 5 4 3 2 1

British Library Cataloguing in Publication Data
A catalogue record for this book is available from the British Library

ISBN 978 1 292 24298 9

Printed in Slovakia by Neografia

Acknowledgements
Content written by Rob Bircher, Sally Clifford, Brian Dowse, Victoria Payne and Kirsty Taylor is included.

The author and publisher would like to thank the following individuals and organisations for permission to reproduce photographs:

Getty Images: Keystone/ Hulton Archive 1, Popperfoto 16, Pictorial Parade/ Archive Photos 21, Corbis Historical/ Historical 22, **Alamy Stock Photo:** Ian Dagnall 4, Chronicle 7, Lebrecht Music & Arts/ Lebrecht Authors 14, Pictorial Press 8, Keystone Pictures USA 17, World History Archive 19, dpa picture alliance 20, CTK/Skocovsky Milan 25, **Solo Syndication:** Associated Newspapers Ltd 30,31,39 **National Archives:** U.S. Information Agency. (8/1/1953 – 4/1/1978) 38.

Text Credits:

P39: Chartwell Trust: adapted from Winston Churchill's The Sinews of Peace ('Iron curtain') speech delivered in Fulton, Missouri, USA on 5 March 1946. https://winstonchurchill.org/resources/speeches/1946-1963-elder-statesman/the-sinews-of-peace/ Used with permission from Chartwell Trust;
PP31,33,34: Cold War International History Project: Novikov, Nikolai, 'Telegram from Nikolai Novikov, Soviet Ambassador to the US, to the Soviet Leadership 27/09/46, History and Public Policy Program Digital Archive, AVP SSSR, f. 06. op. 8, p. 45, p. 759', (c) 1946. History and Public Policy Program Digital Archive, http://digitalarchive.wilsoncenter.org/document/110808 Cold War International History Project

Note from the publisher
Pearson has robust editorial processes, including answer and fact checks, to ensure the accuracy of the content in this publication, and every effort is made to ensure this publication is free of errors. We are, however, only human, and occasionally errors do occur. Pearson is not liable for any misunderstandings that arise as a result of errors in this publication, but it is our priority to ensure that the content is accurate. If you spot an error, please do contact us at resourcescorrections@pearson.com so we can make sure it is corrected.